Acclaim for
Managing Service Excellence

"Rarely do you find a book that has everything, but C. William Crutcher hits on all six cylinders with *Managing Service Excellence*! Through story-telling, practical examples and end-of-chapter reviews, Crutcher skillfully imparts his extensive knowledge on the important topic of customer service. This is a must read for anyone, regardless of industry, who interfaces directly or indirectly with their organization's customers."

—Kellie J. Sigh, Director, Milwaukee Public Schools

"In an era where interpersonal communication and customer care often lag behind technology, *Managing Service Excellence* is a pragmatic and insightful resource for understanding what constitutes, as well as how to deliver, first-class service. Crutcher breaks the concept into actionable parts and provides a practical approach for building and implementing quality standards and sustainable service models."

—Erin Blecha-Ward, Director of Fan Experience, Atlanta Hawks Basketball Club

"This book is the definitive comprehensive and insightful training guide for companies and individuals striving to deliver and sustain outstanding customer service. Crutcher has captured all the complexities involved in the customer service process and presents it in an easy-to-read and instructional format. A must-read resource book!"

—Reginald J. Baron, Director, Mobile Sales, MTA New York City Transit

Managing
Service Excellence

The Ultimate Guide to Building and
Maintaining a Customer-Centric Organization

C. William Crutcher

DIAMIN PUBLISHING

Cover and interior design by Pam Germer, quadegraphiqs.com
Editing by Nivi Nagiel, finalcopy.biz
Author photograph by Pamela Cather, reflectetc.com

All images copyright by the author or have been licensed by the author, unless otherwise noted.

Although the author and publisher have taken every precaution in the preparation of this book, the author and publisher do not assume and hereby disclaim any liability to any party for any loss, damage, or disruption caused by errors or omissions, or resulting from the use of the information contained herein.

Paperback ISBN 978-0-692-98571-7
First edition 2017

For

Diane, Amie, Mike, Mindie, Autumn & Carson

&

*every person committed
to putting the customer—internal and external—first*

Contents

Foreword by Fernando Flores   xiii

Introduction   xv

Chapter 1: Foundations of Customer Service   1

Importance of Customers   1

A Customer-Centric Culture   2

     Living a Culture of Service   3

The Root of Service: Attitude, Knowledge and Empowerment   4

Who Are Your Customers?   6

     View of Customers   7

Seven Myths of Customer Service   8

     Myth #1: Customers Are an Interruption   8

     Myth #2: Customers Have to Do Business with You   9

     Myth #3: Products and Services Alone Create Customer Loyalty   9

     Myth #4: Customers Will Remain Loyal Over Time   11

     Myth #5: Your Service Is Compared Only to Others in Similar Industries   12

     Myth #6: To Your Customers, You Represent Only a Fraction of the Company   12

     Myth #7: The Customer Is Always Right   13

Customers Do Leave—Never to Return   14

Customer Wants vs. Needs   17

Chapter Review Questions   18

Chapter 2: Drivers of Human Behavior   22

We Are All Icebergs   22

Needs   23

Personality   26

Values   29

Knowledge   31

What You Are Is Where You Were When   31

Conclusion   35

Chapter Review Questions   36

Chapter 3: Planning   **40**

We Plan a Lot   40

Why We Plan   41

Organizational Planning   43

Successful People and Organizations Expected to Be   43

Strategic Planning Matrix   43

Strategic Components   43

Tactical/Operational Components   46

"Line of Sight"   47

No or Incomplete Planning   47

Chapter Review Questions   50

Chapter 4: Effective Communication Strategies   **54**

Why We Communicate   54

Interpersonal Communication Process   55

Why Communication Breaks Down   57

Noise: Barriers to Effective Communication   58

Communication Styles   60

Communication Types or Mediums   62

Nonverbal Communication   64

Voice Inflection   65

Rate of Speech   66
Listening   66
    Listen More Than You Speak   67
Chapter Review Questions   69

Chapter 5: Effective Teaming   **72**
We Are Not Alone   72
    Why We Join Teams   72
    Group Versus Team   73
The BIG "C" in Teaming Is Commitment!   74
    The Essentials of Effective Teaming   74
    Types of Teams   76
    Team Development   77
    Norms   78
      No One Washes a Rental Car   79
    Being an Effective Team Member   79
Chapter Review Questions   81

Chapter 6: Effective Coaching   **85**
Understanding Coaching   85
When Employees Grow, So Does Your Number of Customers   85
    Roles of Coaching   85
    Qualities of Successful Coaches 89
    Employee Coaching Steps   90
    Benefits of Coaching   90
Chapter Review Questions   91

Chapter 7: Managing Change   **95**
Overview   95

How Change Is Rejected   96
Managing During Rejection   97
Managing During Reconciliation   97
Managing During Acceptance   98
Regression   99
Conclusion   99
Chapter Review Questions   100

Chapter 8: Critical Thinking and Problem-Solving   **104**
Overview   104
Common Descriptions   104
Characteristics of Critical Thinkers   105
Barriers   106
Problems   107
Problem Discovery and Approach   107
Prioritizing   109
Problem-Solving Process   110
Step 1: Define the Problem   110
Writing the Problem Statement   111
Data Gathering   112
Process Flow Mapping   112
Step 2: Problem Analysis   113
Gap Analysis   114
Root Cause Analysis   114
Cause & Effect (Fishbone) Diagram   115
Force Field Analysis   116
Step 3: Solve   117
Solution Selection Considerations   118
Conclusion   119

Chapter Review Questions   120

Chapter 9: Measuring Customer Satisfaction   **123**
Overview   123
    The Importance of Customer Satisfaction   123
Learning What the Customer Thinks   124
    Comment Cards   124
    Mystery or Secret Shoppers   125
    Focus Groups   126
    Customer Complaints   126
    Employee Feedback   127
    Customer Surveys   128
    Service Metrics   128
Conclusion   130
Chapter Review Questions   131

Chapter 10: Sexual Harassment   **135**
Overview   135
    Legal Definition   135
    Sexual Harassment and Federal Law   136
    Simple Guideline   136
Why People Engage in Sexually Harassing Conduct   136
Importance of Sexual Harassment Training   137
Sexual Harassment Categories   137
    Quid Pro Quo Sexual Harassment   137
      Quid Pro Quo Example   138
    Hostile Environment Sexual Harassment   139
      Hostile Work Environment Example 139
      Victims of Hostile Work Environment Sexual Harassment 140

Topics and Words to Avoid   141
Third-Party Sexual Harassment   141
    Third-Party Example   141
Reporting Sexual Harassment   142
Conclusion   143
Chapter Review Questions   144

Chapter 11: Business Ethics   **148**
Overview   148
    Definition of Ethics   149
Importance of Ethics Training   150
Reporting Unethical Behavior   150
Practicing Ethical Behavior   151
Chapter Review Questions   152

Chapter Review Questions: Answer Grid   **155**

Acknowledgments   **161**

Foreword

I had the pleasure and honor of meeting Bill Crutcher in Orlando, Florida, at the 2016 Annual Conference of the National Customer Service Association, over which he presides. Bill is an inspirational leader and true subject matter expert in the dynamic and increasingly important field of customer service management. I have enormous respect for Bill's deep understanding of human dynamics and organizational planning, and how he applies those to customer service. In fact, he has received numerous accolades for his ability to bond teams and motivate diverse work groups. Noticeable achievements throughout his career include the development of proprietary managerial models, some of which, like the "AKE," are discussed in this book.

We both share a passion for true service excellence, which stems not only from the inherent managerial challenges that striving for excellence will bring, but also from the satisfaction of doing what's right for the people we care about. Said another way, doing the right thing to help others is a meaningful endeavor, one that should make all of us customer service professionals proud of what we do every day.

In my current leadership role at Universal Parks & Resorts Vacations™, my team and I take our commitment to building a customer-focused organization very seriously. We spend a significant amount of our daily lives strategizing on how to deliver excellent service to all of our resort guests. It's not an easy undertaking, and as fortunate as we are to be building off of a very strong business culture here at Universal Orlando Resort™— one in which our team members are extremely engaged—managing for service excellence requires the mastery of many skill sets, on top of solid business values and a customer-experience strategy.

This book zeroes in on those skills customer service professionals in any organization need to focus on in order to be successful. It's easy for businesses today to chase the shiny new penny and look only to technology to deliver innovative customer experiences. It is important to keep in mind that technology should only be a tool that helps enable customer experiences, and that technology alone can never take the place of core competencies every organization should have when it comes to delivering on their brand promise. Many organizations today would certainly benefit from going back to basics and refocusing on strengthening those skill sets needed to more effectively plan, communicate, collaborate, coach, measure success and create a business culture that fosters diversity, inclusion and integrity.

I believe that all customer service professionals should, regardless of role and tenure, read *Managing Service Excellence* to both remind us of why we are in business in the first place and to know what to focus on should we want to remain relevant to our customers. Look around the business landscape today and you'll find that the next competitive battle amongst companies is taking place in the customer experience arena. How can you change what you do today to make the service you provide better, faster and more cost-effective to your customers? Think about what needs to change in your organization so you can disrupt your competitors through better service.

Driving the changes you need to enhance the customer experience may well be the single most important thing you and your organization should focus on to remain competitive. This, however, requires teamwork and a solid change-management plan to ensure success. Many times organizations will look to the frontline customer service teams to resolve pain points in the customer journey without really understanding the root cause. Often, upstream dysfunctions remain unnoticed or unresolved, causing stress on the frontline service teams. I believe you will find a very useful framework in this book to help your organization collaborate and hone in on the problems impacting your ability to deliver excellent service. Enjoy the book!

Fernando Flores
Vice President, Universal Orlando Resort
September 2017

Introduction

The most successful companies have dedicated employees, produce highly desired products and services and maintain a loyal customer base. But while your employees may be the best and brightest, and your products and services the greatest, without customers, you do not exist. Period. Unlike the movie *Field of Dreams,* if you build it, they may NOT come. Thus, in any industry, attracting and retaining customers is *the* primary job of every business.

One might argue that for public organizations, a customer focus is not important because they are "the only game in town." Though some government employees may hold this attitude, at any point there may emerge another alternative—competition (e.g., outsourcing). Treating your customers so they *want to*—not *have to*—do business with you is always the strategy for long-term business success. The customer emphasis this book encourages applies to all organizations, private and public.

This book focuses on the skills required to consistently deliver and manage excellence in customer service. By design, it is not a step-by-step outline, but instead explores the diverse topics integral to providing effective customer service. It is written for anyone committed to putting the customer first—from the frontline customer service representative to the leader dedicated to developing and sustaining that all-important customer-centric culture.

As you read the following pages, remember these words, attributed to Mahatma Gandhi:

> *A customer is the most important visitor on our premises. He is not dependent on us. We are dependent on him. He is not an interruption in our work. He is the purpose of it. He is not an outsider in our business. He is part of it. We are not doing him*

a favor by serving him. He is doing us a favor by giving us an opportunity to do so.

Use this book to consistently achieve service excellence.

CHAPTER 1

Foundations of Customer Service

Importance of Customers

Without customers, you do not have an enterprise. Obvious as this may seem, we don't always behave in a mode of customer service excellence. Simply stated, customers are the reason you are in business. Yes, various stakeholders may rely on your business, including employees, stockholders, the community and others. But the primary and most essential stakeholder is your customer. Without their present and anticipated repeat business, your organization has little viability and no sustained purpose for being.

It is also important to understand that the customer is your source for improvement and innovation. When you seek and act upon customer feedback, you learn what you are doing well and what needs to improve. It may be advice that a process is cumbersome or inefficient, or it may be an idea for an entirely new product. Listening to your customer, through both formal (e.g., satisfaction surveys) and informal (e.g., ad hoc comments) feedback, will reveal what you need to do to keep them coming back. (In Chapter 9 we will address mechanisms for collecting customer input.)

Customer feedback can also drive the strategic direction of a business. What customers are buying and not buying should influence every organization's decision-making. If you build it, they just may not come. Organizations that are responsive to changing customer wants and expectations will find that providing the same products and services they did just five years ago may not be effective in next year's marketplace.

The bottom line is that businesses exist because of their customers. The wise businessperson knows that the customer makes tomorrow possible, and behaves accordingly every day.

1

A Customer-Centric Culture

All organizations have a primary culture. Larger organizations also have subcultures (e.g., divisions, departments) that, hopefully, support the primary culture. What is a culture? It is the combined behaviors of the employees—behaviors that are both encouraged (planned) and tolerated (not always positive). Cultures can be informal, i.e., undocumented and free-flowing. Employees "learn" such cultures through observation and enforcement or lack thereof. Organizations with clear expectations of employee behaviors, on the other hand, typically document organizational values and supporting behaviors. Employees are educated on these values to ensure they clearly understand how the values are to be reflected in day-to-day work activities. Leadership then reinforces those expectations through routine feedback in the form of goal setting, review and performance evaluation.

On my way one day to the university where I teach, I stopped at a fast-food restaurant for coffee. Waiting in line, I noticed a plaque on the wall that read, "Whatever it takes. We will do whatever it takes to satisfy our customers." I thought it was a visible display of a strong customer-centric culture. When I reached the counter, I asked my order taker what that sign meant—hoping to hear something about an enterprise-wide focus on customers. Her reply was, "I'm not sure, they just hung it up the other day." Organizational values with cultural expectations must include adequate training of all employees on those expectations if behavioral changes are desired.

The focus of an organization's culture can contribute or detract from its overall success. Take for example the company that places client billable hours as the most important measure of overall organizational success. That culture carries the risk that customers, employees and other stake-holders will be shortchanged in the process—not getting what they need and deserve.

If you focus on making money, you will do the wrong thing.
If you focus on doing the right thing, you will make money.
—C. WILLIAM CRUTCHER

A customer-centric focus puts the customer first. This includes the "bill-paying" customer and the "internal" customer—the employees. The organization with a customer focus marshals its resources to not only provide the best products and services, but also to create relationships, assuring the customer they are the reason the company exists. Customers must be valued and never taken for granted. The remainder of this book provides essential practices for creating and maintaining a customer-centric organization.

LIVING A CULTURE OF SERVICE

How can we tell if an organization is "living" a culture of service? There are several associated indicators.

First and foremost, the culture is agile, resilient and principled. It is grounded in shared values that all employees embrace. Achieving and maintaining the desired culture requires that each employee understand the values and how they impact their day-to-day performance.

Leadership turns great strategy into great performance. This means that the organization's mission, vision and values are shared with all employees. Creating "line-of-sight" to the mission, vision and values for all employees is key to sustaining the desired culture.

Promises are kept by all employees. While this sounds simple, one of the greatest sources of employee and customer dissatisfaction is unfulfilled promises. We get busy, overextend ourselves, forget to do something—whatever the reason, it sounds like excuses to the employee or customer. Keep the promises you make. Expectations must be met without excuses.

Every interaction is respectful and efficient—both internally and externally. How often do we give others a pass because they are having a bad day? What if everyone has a bad day? Is total chaos then acceptable? No. Regardless of personal issues, treating others with respect is an "always" condition. That is key to a true culture of service.

Last, we find that communication is clear, concise and consistent. We think about what we want to communicate before doing so. Whatever the nature of the communication, if the recipient doesn't get understandable information, subsequent actions will fall short of expectations.

For example, suppose you ask your handyman to install a swing on your property. Upon arriving home that evening, you find a tire swing hanging from a tree limb in your backyard. But what you wanted was a porch swing. Absent clear information, the deliverable you get may be far different than the one you expect.

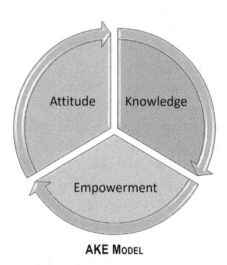

AKE MODEL

The Root of Service: Attitude, Knowledge and Empowerment

Excellence in customer service relies on key precursory conditions. First is an *attitude of service.* True customer service professionals understand that to effectively serve, they must put their own wants and needs behind those of the customer. That is not to say that the customer wins and the company loses, but that the customer is placed first. Imagine a large company parking lot at the close of day. There is chaos as employees struggle to be the next one out, cutting off others in the process. Now imagine if all employees had a "you first, then me" attitude. The picture is calmer and the lot empties more quickly. People go home happier. It is the same with effective customer service. When we employ a "you first, then me" approach to serving, we become better listeners, act more cordially and create relationships that lead to long-term customer loyalty.

A colleague and I went for a late lunch at a local chain restaurant. As we approached the register to place our order, we noticed the employee was focused on whatever she was doing on her cell phone. My colleague cleared his throat to get her attention. She looked up and exaggerated a sigh—her way of letting us know she did not appreciate being interrupted. The notion of an attitude of service was clearly not in her vocabulary, let alone her customer interactions.

The second root of service is *knowledge.* This means knowing your job and knowing it well. Know your products and services and what they can do for the customer. It is also important you understand how your job fits with others in the organization. Whether you are serving a steak, providing a technical report or delivering 10 yards of concrete, your customers rely on you to be the subject matter expert. You ARE the company and you determine the customer's impression of your organization.

Have you ever been to a restaurant where your server appeared to not know their menu? While we should certainly appreciate the learning curve for new employees, it becomes frustrating when the server responds to every inquiry with "Let me check." The server should take the time to learn what's on the menu and what substitutions or modifications can be made. Lack of knowledge about your products or services does not instill confidence in your customers.

The third root of service is *empowerment.* It is frustrating for customers to deal with employees who are not able to resolve service issues. As the customer service professional, it is essential that you know what latitude you have to serve your customers. When there is a service breakdown, do you have to "check with the boss" or are you able to offer alternatives to the customer?

How good does it make you feel as a customer when an employee offers you some reward, on the spot, for a service breakdown? You quickly understand that the business values its customers. Naturally, some organizations allow their employees greater autonomy than others. If empowerment is lacking though, and employees regularly need permission before taking a course of action, the service professional has the opportunity to reflect positive strategies to leadership that will, hopefully, influence greater empowerment.

Who Are Your Customers?

Simply defined,

> **A customer is any person or group to whom you provide a good or service.**

Typically, when we think of a customer, we think of the person or group paying for that service or product. This could be the family receiving their meals at the restaurant, the person getting a car loan at the bank or a business having the roof replaced on their headquarters building. Each transaction involves a product or service and one or more customers.

Your view is likely that those who pay the bills—external customers— are your only true customers. But often disregarded as a customer is the person who works down the hall from you, or in another department or building of your company.

> *If you're not serving the bill-paying customer,*
> *you'd better be serving someone who is!*
> —NUMEROUS ATTRIBUTIONS

6

Every employee has customers, whether external or internal to the organization, or both. If a person does not create something that is or could be used by another, then why would that job exist? The report generated by the finance department, the supplies ordered by the office clerk and even the restrooms cleaned by the custodian all contribute to the marketable outputs of the organization. While some jobs may be more directly linked to the external customer, everyone in the organization must work together effectively to retain that customer-focused competitive advantage.

VIEW OF CUSTOMERS

Ultimately, how you think about your customers shapes how you serve them.

When we think "user," we tend to believe that our obligation is complete when the product or service has been delivered. So, when you deliver your monthly finance report, you have no other responsibility to them until next month. You communicate very little with the "user" between monthly reports. This thinking leads to doing much less for the customer than we are capable of.

When we think "customer," we behave as though our obligation is never really complete. We interact more regularly to ensure the product or service we are delivering meets their needs. If not, we modify our deliverables to maximize their value to our customer and thus increase the value to the end customer. We meet with our customer and share how we can assist them, what schedules we must follow and the flexibility we have to serve them. We also share how they can be a better customer—what they can do for us that will help us support them.

So, while viewing the external bill-paying customer as our sole customer may seem intuitive, we must recognize the vital importance of our internal customers as well. Adopting this broadened perspective of customers enhances our interactions and deliverables, and results in a more successful organization overall.

Seven Myths of Customer Service

In our trainings and dealings with individuals from various organizations and industries, it is not unusual to hear some shared beliefs—often un-founded—about customers. Some are accurate; others are what we term customer *myths.*

What is a myth? It is a widely held, but false, belief or idea. As we grow up and gain ex-perience, we find that many stories we believed as children prove inaccurate. The field of cus-tomer service contains its own myths, and they can affect how we relate to and build relation-ships with customers. The customer service pro-fessional can learn much from these myths.

Following are popular customer myths:

MYTH #1: CUSTOMERS ARE AN INTERRUPTION

The reality is that customers are NEVER an interruption. They are the reason your business exists. Without them, your organization serves no purpose.

Imagine you are attempting to accomplish a certain task and just need a little more time to finish. Then, lo and behold, in comes a customer. What bad timing. Do you think your attitude at that moment may be felt by the customer? Words, vocal tone or nonverbals are likely to ex-pose your feelings.

Customers are NEVER an interruption. Let me say this again: CUS-TOMERS ARE NEVER AN INTERRUPTION! They drive improve-ment and innovation. Think about the many products that exist today because of customers. It is their feedback—if we wisely listen and use it—that allows businesses to adjust products and services and how they are delivered. Look at Coca-Cola's Freestyle® soft drink dispenser. Customers kept demanding more options and this machine now delivers over 100 soft drink flavors—each one selected by the customer. Allow yourself to be "interrupted" by your customers and you may be surprised by the positive consequences. The bottom line is that customers make your business's tomorrow possible.

MYTH #2: CUSTOMERS HAVE TO DO BUSINESS WITH YOU

In reality, there are <u>always</u> options. Many people feel free from competition and therefore enjoy job security regardless of customer opinion. Examples could include employees of the accounts payable department in a private business or the street department crew of a municipality. For their customers, there may not currently be an alternative source for those services. In reality, though, these functions could always be provided by a third-party vendor. If you think your job could never be outsourced, you are wrong. Some entity "out there" would love to take on your functions and will lobby your leadership for the opportunity.

In one of my former corporate roles, we were regularly approached by outsourcers—businesses that wanted to do the work our employees were doing. They would always promise better service at cheaper prices. This was not lost on our employees. One day, an employee told me she heard that part or all of the department might be outsourced. Though it was just a rumor, she was concerned about losing her job. What was my coaching? I told her to do her job the best she could. And by doing so, she raised the bar for any outside entity with sights of replacing her.

To ensure your employer would never consider outsourcing your job, do what you do, the very best you can. You must treat your customers so they WANT to do business with you, not because they HAVE TO. Coming to work every day and believing that a competitor wants your customers should cause you to upgrade your service—because it is true!

MYTH #3: PRODUCTS AND SERVICES ALONE CREATE CUSTOMER LOYALTY

The reality is that long-term loyalty is directly impacted by our relationship with the customer. Many businesses once focused on a single business line. For example, if you wanted a refrigerator or dishwasher you went to an appliance store. Now, many companies have multiple product lines—often under the same roof. A refrigerator, dog food and vitamins can all be purchased from a single store. It seems that competition is at every intersection and is continually growing.

Since customers can select from many vendors for the same product, businesses must focus on differentiating themselves by the level of service they provide. Customer service professionals embrace this focus and understand their ability to build loyal relationships with customers through enhanced service. Customers may initially select a business because of its products, prices, proximity and associated service. However, research indicates that prices are often not the primary consideration once the customer has a positive relationship with employees of a particular business.

How does the customer service professional go about creating those treasured positive relationships?

- Begin by always keeping your promises. The key here is to make the promises you can keep and keep the promises you make. This speaks volumes to one's integrity. Breaking promises is a significant contributor to customer dissatisfaction.

  Say, for example, the cable company promised a service technician would be at your residence the next day between 10:00 a.m. and noon. It's mid-afternoon the next day and still no service technician. To add to the issue, you do not even get an update call. The technician shows up at 4 p.m. and says his last job took longer than expected. How does that make you feel? Your trust in the cable company is likely diminished. Do you call the company and share your disappointment or do you share your experience with friends and coworkers? Research suggests you will do the latter.

- Being respectful and respectable are the precursors to respect. Both in and out of the presence of customers—internal and external—speak and behave respectfully toward them. Paraphrasing the late Stephen Covey, do not go to Mary to confess the sins of Larry. That is what we commonly refer to as gossip. It does not contribute to solving issues and certainly not to building positive relationships.

- Maintain a "can-do" attitude. Customers respond positively to service professionals who focus on how something can be done versus why it can't be done. Most often, reasons something cannot be done end up sounding like excuses to the customer.

I was traveling to a conference a few years back and upon arriving late to the hotel, I was informed the room type I had reserved was not available. I indicated that since I would be hosting a business meeting in the room, I really needed the additional space. The manager walked over and the front desk representative quickly apprised him of the situation. When I shared again why I required that additional space, his comment was, "Let me see how I can make that happen for you." What a positive, encouraging response. I did not end up with the exact room type I had originally reserved, but sufficient accommodations for my needs. As with me, most of us put those great service experiences in our memory banks. Likewise do your customers.

- Make regular "pit stops." Check in on your customers between normal interactions. Find out how your product or service is working for them and explore how else you can be of assistance. This provides you the opportunity to build those important relationships, which can otherwise be a struggle during the "heat of the battle."

- Value our differences. It is important to customers that they not be forced into a one-size-fits-all situation. Value what each customer represents to your organization and work to fill their unique needs to the extent possible.

Remember—maintaining positive relationships with your customers is the bona fide competitive business advantage.

MYTH #4: CUSTOMERS WILL REMAIN LOYAL OVER TIME

In reality, customers are NOT yours for a lifetime. They may only be loyal to you or your organization through the NEXT INTERACTION! It may feel like it takes a lifetime to create that coveted customer loyalty, and yet it can take one disconnect and that customer is lost, forever.

Sadly, when a customer leaves, they rarely share why with the business. They will, though, typically tell their friends and colleagues. This is not the type of publicity that any organization desires. It is incumbent upon the customer service professional to maintain the kind of relationships that will weather an occasional breakdown—because they will happen from time to time.

Remember—opportunities are never lost. Someone will take the ones you miss.

MYTH #5: YOUR SERVICE IS COMPARED ONLY TO OTHERS IN SIMILAR INDUSTRIES

The reality is that your competition is ANYONE who raises customer expectations. For example, assume a customer has just brought their car in to a quick-oil-change shop. The employees there were courteous, worked quickly and explained what was done in easy-to-understand terms. The customer leaves with a smile on their face.

Now, the customer comes to your business. The barometer of customer satisfaction is not the comparison to how they were last treated here or at your competitors, but rather at the oil-change facility. The customer will be reflecting on their most recent customer service experience, and consciously or subconsciously comparing you accordingly. Your job is to raise the service bar for the next business.

MYTH #6: TO YOUR CUSTOMERS, YOU REPRESENT ONLY A FRACTION OF THE COMPANY

To the world, you may just be one person.
To one person, you just may be the world.

—HENRY FORD

In reality, to your customers, you ARE the company, regardless of your job description. If you are the point of contact, the customer will expect that you speak and behave on behalf of your company.

As an example, a service technician for a telephone company is handling a service outage in a small rural town. While checking the lines, he is stopped by an elderly gentleman who shows him his telephone bill. The customer says he is confused by all the line items on the bill—taxes, fees, etc. Instead of saying to the gentleman, "Billing is not my job; you will have to contact the office," he says, "I will have someone from our billing department call you to explain the bill details." While the customer is happy—for the moment—it is critical to follow through to make sure promises are kept. That is an "attitude of service" in action. To the customer, the service technician WAS the company and his actions left a positive image of it.

MYTH #7: THE CUSTOMER IS ALWAYS RIGHT

While this maxim has been around for a long time, the reality is that the customer is not, in fact, always right. But, as the customer service professional, your focus is not to show the customer why or how they are wrong. That is a recipe for disaster.

When the customer is wrong, it is important to share that you recognize how they could feel that way. You may find it helpful to use terms such as "I'm sorry, I may not have been clear . . ." The focus must be on moving forward—identifying and implementing a solution to the current issue—not laying blame. Stating something as simple as "Why don't we try this" will likely be well received by the customer and shift the focus from the current breakdown to a mutually acceptable solution.

It is equally important to set the stage for future interactions while equipping the customer with more accurate information. Ending with "The next time we do this, we should . . ." will leave the customer with a positive feeling for the next exchange.

Remember, *being appropriate* is more important than *being right.* The true customer service professional knows that laying blame does nothing for positive long-term relationships. In the end, the goal is a customer willing to remain your customer.

Customers Do Leave—Never to Return

Regardless of best efforts, customers do leave businesses. According to Michael LeBoeuf in his book *How to Win Customers and Keep Them for Life*, the following reasons are attributed to customer departure:

- 3% moved and the business was no longer easily accessible.
- 5% developed other relationships that attracted the customer's business.
- 9% left for competitive reasons; the customer found better products or service with another provider.
- 14% were dissatisfied with the product or service.
- 68% left *because of an attitude of indifference toward the customer by the owner, manager or other employee.*

This should be an eye-opener: Most customers left because of how they were treated! It is estimated that businesses spend six to seven times more to acquire a new customer than to retain a current one. These statistics suggest that a vast improvement in customer retention efforts, including regular employee training, is critical to business success.

Customer dissatisfaction is associated with the following primary contributing factors:

- *A promise that was not delivered on.* Refer back to the example of the cable technician. Not showing up when expected was a cause for frustration and a strained relationship with the company. Again, we must make the promises we can keep and keep the promises we make.

- *Service that was rude or inefficient.* Treat every customer as though you want them to return—because you do! They are the reason you are in business, and they can choose to go elsewhere—"vote with their feet."

- *Conflicting messages from different employees.* It is important that all customer-contact employees understand the organization's procedures and communicate them consistently to customers.

In one of my corporate jobs, I traveled frequently. Twenty-four hours before departure, we could call the airline for an upgrade to first class based on availability. This became a bit of a game. If the agent indicated there was no space available, we would hang up and call right back. We always got a different agent, and in many cases, there would magically be upgrade space available. It was clear that some agents did not understand the procedure, or worse, chose not to process the upgrade. Either way, the inconsistency did not leave a positive image of their training and commitment to the customer.

- *Being taken advantage of, or having the feeling of being taken advantage of.* You may be the expert in your field, but remember, your customer probably isn't.

Imagine you are driving on the highway and there appears to be excessive vibration at higher speeds. You take the car to a service center for diagnostics and repair. The service technician says you have a blown front passenger strut and the repair will be $495. He further states that while they do that repair, they will rotate and balance your tires at no charge. Is this a good deal? You probably don't know. It could be that all you really needed was your tires balanced to eliminate the vibration. Or, possibly you did have a bad strut. Because we are not subject matter experts in most things, it is incumbent upon the service professional to take time to explain their products and services to the customer and make sure all questions are answered in understandable terms.

- *Delays and long waits to receive products or services.* For example, if you anticipate that a product is going to be back-ordered, tell your customer up front. If your restaurant has an unexpectedly large number of diners one evening and you haven't staffed accordingly, share that there may be a slight delay in food delivery. You might offer a complimentary drink or appetizer to show appreciation for the customer's patience. Bottom line: It is extremely important to manage customer expectations.

- *Defective or inferior products or services—unfulfilled expectations.* A guarantee doesn't mean that a product won't break or that all promises will be fulfilled precisely as stated—no matter how hard a company may try. The key is how you handle that breakdown with the customer. What are you doing to minimize the impact on them? Do you deliver that replacement lawn mower or offer a complimentary meal? Things will go wrong. How you recover is what matters.

- *Lack of communication—not knowing what is happening and thus thinking the worst.*

  In another travel situation several years ago, our airplane pushed back from the gate at a major international airport and we sat on the taxiway for three very long hours. During that time, we received but a single update from the cockpit. To say that the passengers were upset would be putting it mildly. The key for any business is that when there are unforeseen delays, provide regular updates to your customers.

- *Being dishonest—also known as "business suicide."* This one is simple. Tell the truth, even if it may not be what the customer wants to hear. Lying is the highest form of disrespect, and in certain situations could result in legal consequences.

The customer service professional understands that customers can and will leave the business under certain conditions. The role of the service professional and the business is to do what is necessary to prevent, or at least minimize, those conditions.

Customer Wants vs. Needs

While customers will tell us what they want, we must often decipher their actual needs. It has been said that if Henry Ford gave customers what they *wanted* instead of what they *needed,* he would have invested in faster horses. Thus, it is important to recognize and remember what customers both "want" and "need."

In summary, what do customers actually need?

- Specific products and services
- Options—recognizing this is not a one-size-fits-all world
- Clear and timely communication
- Positive, supportive relationships with business points of contact
- Understanding of their particular situation
- Reliable partnership—one that can be counted on in every interaction, every time

While customers may say they want specific products or services, their actual wants can be expressed in the following statement:

Customers want their needs met to their satisfaction, not yours or the business's; on their timetable, not yours; while being treated in a fair and respectful manner.

This statement is much easier said than acted upon.

In summary, a mastery of these foundations of customer service— knowing and living them every day—is essential to the long-term success of ANY business. It is important to fully appreciate the value of your customers—not just in the revenue they provide today—but the promise they hold for your business tomorrow and beyond.

Chapter Review Questions

1. An organization's most essential stakeholder is its:
   a. Stockholders
   b. Community
   c. Employees
   d. Customers

2. Customers can drive the strategic direction of an organization.
   a. True
   b. False

3. An organizational culture that focuses on the customer is said to be:
   a. Service-oriented
   b. Customer-centric
   c. Business-centric
   d. Community-minded

4. All but which of the following indicate that an organization is living a culture of service?
   a. Shared values are understood by all employees.
   b. Employees accept that all promises cannot be delivered upon.
   c. Interactions are respectful.
   d. Communication is clear and consistent.

5. The root elements of service include:
   a. Attitude, knowledge and determination
   b. Planning, communication and power
   c. Attitude, knowledge and empowerment
   d. Knowledge, skills and support

6. Which of the following is a customer?
   a. A coworker who asks you how to use the copy machine
   b. A diner in your restaurant
   c. An employee in another department of your company who receives your monthly operating report
   d. a & b
   e. a & c
   f. b & c
   g. a, b & c

7. Thinking of internal customers as "users" allows us to more effectively serve them.
   a. True
   b. False

8. There are often positive consequences to being "interrupted" by a customer.
   a. True
   b. False

9. When you feel your organization has a monopoly on what you provide your customers:
   a. Securing customer feedback on your products or services is not essential.
   b. You should consider limiting direct customer interaction times.
   c. Job security is no longer an issue for you or your employees.
   d. Your job functions may be more easily assumed by a third-party vendor.

10. All but which of the following are necessary for maintaining customer loyalty?
    a. Following up with your customers only when you are contacted by them
    b. Keeping your promises
    c. Maintaining a positive, can-do approach
    d. Treating customers uniquely

11. Once customers become loyal to you or your organization, they are typically your customers for a lifetime.
    a. True
    b. False

12. To your customers, you are the company, regardless of your actual job duties.
    a. True
    b. False

13. It is a falsehood that the customer is always right; therefore, when the customer is actually wrong, you should:
    a. Let the customer know why they were in error.
    b. Advise the customer you are very knowledgeable regarding this situation.
    c. Tell the customer to not try that same approach in the future.
    d. Focus on moving forward with a solution and not laying blame.

14. The primary reason customers leave businesses is that they:
    a. Got a better deal somewhere else
    b. Were treated with indifference by the owner, manager or an employee
    c. Moved away from the area
    d. Were dissatisfied with the product or service

15. Customers need all but which of the following?
    a. Clear and timely communication
    b. The lowest prices for products and services
    c. Positive, supportive relationships with business points of contact
    d. Understanding of their particular situation

CHAPTER 2

Drivers of Human Behavior

We Are All Icebergs

Understanding what drives customer behavior, as well as our own, is extremely helpful in delivering effective customer service. While the study of human behavior is a complex discipline, let's simplify it through the iceberg model.

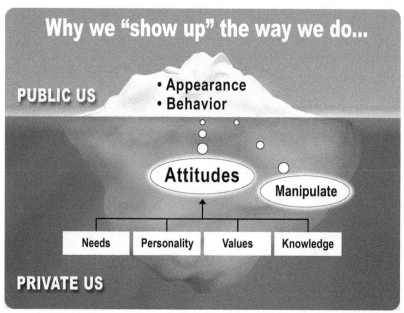

ICEBERG MODEL

As the model shows, like the iceberg, the visible or "public" part of us is a small portion of the whole. That public portion—what those around us see—includes *appearance* and *behavior.* Usually, we judge others based on these two dimensions, though we may know little, if anything, about them. When this happens, what we are doing is evaluating others based on our paradigms—our own life experiences—and often that assessment is wrong.

To fully appreciate another person, we have to go beneath the surface—attempt to understand the "why" of their behaviors. As the model suggests, that "private" portion is the much larger part and requires our authentic effort to discern.

Behaviors are driven by our attitudes toward people, places and things. The stronger our attitudes, the more consistent the behaviors. For example, a nonsmoker doesn't have to "think" about not lighting up a cigarette. They have an attitude against smoking and thus don't have to consciously think about not smoking. On the other hand, some people work hard to lose 20 pounds and then soon thereafter regain the weight. Why is this? They manipulated their behavior—consciously thinking about eating lower calorie, healthier foods. But they did not change their attitude toward diet and nutrition. The more automatic behavior is to eat the foods that caused the weight gain in the first place.

Bottom line: We can change our attitudes given the knowledge and motivation to do so.

Attitudes are developed based on four primary factors: *needs, personality, values* and *knowledge.* It is important to understand that while we may be "prewired" (born) with certain needs and personality traits, our experiences over time will impact our overall attitudes, both positively and negatively. Let's explore each of these.

NEEDS

Every human being has needs. Some are *innate*—needs we are born with, e.g., the need for food and warmth. This explains why a newborn baby quickly begins to suckle for nourishment or snuggles closely with its mother. Other needs are developed over time—these are known as *acquired* needs. While there are countless acquired needs, the ones that will best help us understand our customers include:

- *Need for Esteem:* People have a need to feel good about who they are and to be respected. Esteem is the human desire to be not only accepted but valued by others. Helping the customer feel good about themselves every interaction is an excellent relationship-building opportunity.

  Take for example a store that boldly advertises that 5 percent of all sales will go to support U.S. military veterans. While this is certainly considered good "corporate citizenship," the customer feels good—increased esteem—knowing they are supporting a worthwhile cause.

- *Need for Affiliation:* Individuals with a need for affiliation enjoy social relationships and have a need to belong. People in this category respond well to personal attention and supportive behavior. They tend to reach out to others with encouragement and are often eager to please. As a customer, this individual is often willing to work for and accept alternatives. The downside is that their proclivity to social interaction can detract from focusing on the issue at hand.

  In a customer-service-training course one day, a student indicated that every month, a particular elderly customer would call her to discuss his bill. She said that the first couple of times, she was frustrated because he kept asking the same questions. But she soon realized it wasn't his bill that was important; it was the conversation they had. She discovered he had no family, and this monthly call was a chance to connect with a familiar voice and someone who treated him with respect and care.

- *Need for Achievement:* The person with a high need for achievement likes to solve problems. They are motivated by winning and they like rewards—for what they represent, not necessarily the reward itself. These individuals may be both a blessing and a curse for the customer service professional. On one hand, they are not deterred by a challenge, but on the other hand, may want to work toward a solution that is excessive.

Imagine you call a customer because they did not accurately complete your company's online order form. All you require is a little additional information. On the phone, the customer goes into great detail regarding how you could modify the form, and provides several process-improvement recommendations. The customer likely wasn't concerned with "fixing" the form and process for themselves, but felt a sense of achievement by sharing their depth of knowledge.

- *Need for Power:* People with a high need for power like to be in control and respond well when addressed formally. They tend to be punctual and prefer things well organized and explained. When working with such people, the customer service professional must particularly focus on being "correct" versus being "right." A "you first, then me" approach is often effective.

Recently, I was flying home from a client engagement and waited an extraordinarily long time at the airline check-in while another passenger spoke with the agent. He was very loud and demanding. He insisted that the "lady he spoke to on the phone" guaranteed he was booked on a flight, yet his reservation was not in the airline's system. He was verbose and taking a lot of time. The airline employee remained polite, used a soft voice and addressed him as "Mr." in their conversation. Ultimately, she found a seat for him and apologized for any inconvenience. She went the extra mile to not prove that the customer, in this case, may have been wrong.

Most people develop some level of all of the acquired needs above, and, dependent upon the situation, one or more may appear dominantly—and drive behavior. For the customer service professional, this is important to understand so you can watch for signs of the needs at play.

It is the desire to satisfy needs that motivates people to act. Motivation theory indicates that a person will exert themselves to achieve an objective if it satisfies a need. For example, if someone is hungry, they will make the effort to find food so it can satisfy their hunger. Customers put forth effort to get what they feel they need, and the strength of that perceived need determines their commitment to satisfying it. Acknowledging this reality allows us to better understand, and thus satisfy, the needs of the customer.

It is important to recognize that when a customer indicates what they "need," it may well be a "want." In other words, what the customer *thinks* they need is really what they want. These could be two entirely different things, and one may be more realistic to fulfill than the other. Your role—much like a doctor—is to diagnose and prescribe what the customer *actually* needs. This can be challenging, but becomes easier with experience.

When attempting to satisfy customer needs, it is equally important to satisfy the needs of the business as well. Thus, the outcome of customer interaction should result in a <u>win</u> for the customer *and* a <u>win</u> for the company. This approach provides for customer loyalty and long-term success for the organization.

PERSONALITY

Each of us has a personality. Simply defined,

> **Personality is a combination of psychological traits that describe a person and influence behavior.**

Many business professionals have completed some form of personality assessment during their careers. While there are several instruments on the market for assessing personality, we prefer the Myers-Briggs Type Indicator (MBTI), as it is widely used, and the terminology is readily understood.

The MBTI breaks down personality into four pairs of *preferences:*

- *Extraversion (E) vs. Introversion (I)*
- *Sensing (S) vs. Intuition (N)*
- *Thinking (T) vs. Feeling (F)*
- *Judging (J) vs. Perceiving (P)*

Extraversion (E) and Introversion (I) describe our preference for social interaction.

- *Extraversion:* Extraverts tend to be energized by being around people. They enjoy the engagement and experience loneliness when not in contact with others. Customers who are extraverted can be more talkative and may want to continue communicating beyond the time necessary to address the issue. Often referred to as "ready-fire-aim," Extraverts may jump to a conclusion before they have all the requisite information. A good approach to assure important facts, details and options were not missed is to conclude conversations with a summary of next steps, responsible parties and timing.

- *Introversion:* Introverts find their energy sapped when around people. They typically seek quiet time in order to recharge their batteries. Customers who are more introverted are excellent listeners. They think through issues quite well, but can be hesitant to move toward closure. It is not uncommon for an Introvert to backtrack and review earlier points in a conversation. It is the customer service professional's responsibility to ensure sufficient detail is provided to allow closure for this customer.

Sensing (S) and Intuition (N) address how we gather data.

- *Sensing:* The Sensor relies on experience and data for decision-making. This individual is practical and pays attention to details. Since a Sensor tends to make few factual errors, the customer service professional must ensure they have correct information readily available. The customer service professional may find it more tedious to work with this customer because of the detail level expected. On the other hand, engaging this type of customer will encourage the customer service professional to maintain high skill levels and preparedness.

- *Intuition:* While the Sensor may be considered an inside-the-box thinker, the Intuitive is more likely to say, "What box?" They rely on possibilities and inspiration, focus on the big picture and readily work with complex issues. An Intuitive will often recommend viable solutions to an issue, which can be a challenge for the customer service professional, as those solutions may not be available or may be too costly to implement. Once again, the customer service professional must find the balance that meets both the customer's and the organization's needs.

Thinking (T) and Feeling (F) regard our approach to decision-making.

- *Thinking:* The Thinker tends to base decisions on logic. This individual is typically straightforward, brief and businesslike. There can appear to be little room for niceties, as they tend to act impersonally and may seem a little cold or standoffish. The Thinker is a good problem-solver, which makes them a great ally to the customer service professional, though building a warm relationship can be challenging.

- *Feeling:* The Feeler often bases decisions on values and perceived needs of others. They are supportive in dealings and tend to be naturally friendly. They work to ensure the needs of all concerned are satisfied to the extent possible. For the customer service professional, it is easier to build an ongoing relationship with a Feeler. However, this customer may also present a challenge, since they may detract from solving problems, favoring instead to support others.

Judging (J) and Perceiving (P) concern our approach to people and tasks.

- *Judging:* The Judger is typically planful—decisive and self-regimented. They make decisions easily, while focusing on closure—completing the task. They are well organized and contribute to finding solutions in a timely manner, which is a great asset to the customer service professional. Because of this customer's planning and organizational skills, the customer service professional must be detail-oriented in their interactions with a Judger.

- *Perceiving:* The Perceiver is tolerant and spontaneous. They may struggle with details and tend to seek more data, delaying decisions longer than the customer service professional would like. This customer often puts things off until the last minute, which makes closure on issues difficult. It is important that the customer service professional do more hand-holding to ensure the customer has what they need, recognizing

28

the Perceiver may feel uneasy even after a decision is made.

It is important to remember that there are no bad personalities, and that personalities point out *tendencies* in groups of people—not absolutes for anyone. Lastly, individuals *control* their personalities, and not vice versa. A great example of this is the Introvert—who professes discomfort with public speaking—delivering an excellent address to a large crowd.

VALUES

During the formative years of our youth, we develop a sense of what is right, what is wrong and what is important to us. We do this based on our interactions with those around us. Family, friends and even strangers can influence our personal value systems.

> **Values are the central truths, laws or beliefs from which arise the social rules of conduct.**

As drivers of behavior, our values determine how we treat one another and, equally important, ourselves. The strength of these values determines our adherence to them and the stress we experience when we violate them.

A list of one's values can be lengthy. When we work with clients to develop a "shared values" list, it is not unusual for a focus group to brainstorm 30–40 value terms. From the customer service professional's perspective, there are three foundational values that influence bidirectional customer interactions:

- *Respect:* When we truly respect someone, we treat them in a manner that makes them feel good about themselves—in a positive, supportive manner—both in *and* out of their presence. We think in terms of being respectful and respectable—respectful in our actions toward others, and respectable in how our behaviors cause others to treat us. It is often said that when we disrespect another, we have first disrespected ourselves—in other words, violated our personal values. Customers who feel respected will return.

- *Honesty:* Honesty is treating others with fairness and truthfulness. Customers expect—and should demand—honesty from businesses. Once they feel a sense of untruthfulness (a lie, manipulation, not sharing needed information, etc.), the likelihood of that customer returning is remote. People are better equipped to deal with the truth—regardless of its content—than some fiction concocted to make them feel better. A word of caution about being "brutally honest": Unfortunately, the emphasis can shift to *brutal* and the recipient doesn't perceive the *honest* part. Thus, a respectful conversation is always a must.

- *Trust/Integrity:* Trust and integrity go hand in hand. People trust someone who displays integrity. The root of these two values is simply doing what you committed to doing. An excellent definition of integrity for the customer service professional is:

  Doing what you say you will do, even when no one is watching, regardless of the cost.

  Or in other words, *make the promises you can keep and keep the promises you make.* Many of us have been victims of a promise that was not fulfilled. We were promised a product or service on a specific date and it was not delivered. At that point, any *reason* sounds like an empty *excuse.* When it comes from a customer service professional, it can destroy customer loyalty. In reality, there may be valid reasons a commitment cannot be fulfilled. It is incumbent upon the customer service professional to know this at the earliest opportunity and to communicate the status as soon as possible to the customer. Remember, people often give trust as a gift . . . the first time. Once violated, work is required to earn it back—if the customer is willing.

Values are not a sometimes, "when it's convenient" thing. These principles govern behavior 24/7. The good news is that we can work to strengthen our values and their positive influence on our behavior.

KNOWLEDGE

The last factor influencing our attitudes that we will discuss is knowledge.

> **Knowledge is gained in the process of doing and experiencing things.**

We each have a unique set of experiences and thus our knowledge differs. And our knowledge and experiences shape our attitudes. Imagine the difference in experiences between a person growing up in a middle-class home with two nurturing parents, and another raised in poverty by a single parent or grandparent. What each of them knows, understands and believes can be vastly different. And though we may interact with them every day, because we cannot see *beneath the surface,* we don't know the experiences they have endured.

While our previous examples suggest longer-term influences on behavior, what about the customer who just left another business, where they were treated with the highest level of professionalism, respect and courtesy? You will be judged not based upon your last interaction with that customer, but their last interaction—as different as that business may be.

These drivers of behavior should be considered when interacting with customers. It is incumbent upon the customer service professional to create a positive experience for every customer, every interaction. That is what will keep them coming back.

What You Are Is Where You Were When

The drivers of human behavior we just explored impact every person—regardless of age. The nature of our needs, personality and values is greatly influenced by our experiences. Viewing these experiential influences in terms of generation can be helpful, assuming that individuals from the same generation were likely exposed to similar influences. While generational studies vary, most define four generations. More recent studies have included a fifth generation, referred to as "Generation Z."

Generation	Born
Traditionals/Matures	1930–1945
Baby Boomers	1946–1963
Generation X	1964–1981
Millennials	1982–1995
Generation Z	1996–Present

Research suggests that our values, needs and even personalities are shaped largely by the experiences of our formative years—typically through age 12. Some current studies indicate they can extend up to age 25, though for our purposes, we will consider formative years to end approximately with age 12.

An article written many years ago by Morris Massey, entitled "What You Are Is Where You Were When," argues just this—that what we were exposed to during our formative years determines in large part who we are today. Examples of key influencers include:

- Formative events: wars, the Space Race, technological advances, 9/11
- Heroes: sports figures, musicians, presidents, parents
- Television shows: Lawrence Welk, Andy Griffith, *The Simpsons,* reality TV
- Spending styles: save and pay, buy now and pay later, purchase online
- Technology: single-line dial phone, cell phone, texting, Facebook

What does this mean for the customer service professional? Here are some considerations for each generational group:

Traditionals/Matures: Relationships are particularly important and integrity is an absolute. They show a high level of brand loyalty and thus expect that the "brand" will be loyal to them. Their preference is "brick and mortar" and not "click and order"—they like to see and feel what they are purchasing. Desire to use technology is limited. Payment is typically "in full" and they are not particularly impressed with credit card deals. They focus more on needs than wants.

Tips for dealing with traditionals/matures:

- Recognize they tend toward "technophobia" (fear of technology). Provide ample information, necessary instruction and allow for a possible adjustment period.
- Be flexible with additional time it may take them to accept change.
- Show respect for their experience to help foster a strong working relationship.
- Consider them valued partners, and they will be eager to share their knowledge and experience with others. We can learn a great deal from them.

Baby Boomers: This group likes traditional media and is more comfortable with technology. Often, appearances are important. They may have a "he who dies with the most toys wins" mentality. Baby boomers tend to like quick fixes to problems—the easier the better. They are comfortable paying on credit and often find "0%" financing offers appealing. This group can be more inclined to satisfy their *wants* versus their *needs.*

Tips for dealing with baby boomers:

- Offer recognition and rewards for their business.
- Take your time—be friendly and get to know them.
- Recognize their tendency to play phone tag—initiate face-to-face interactions when possible.
- Boomers do not require formal signs of respect, but they do want to know their experience is respected.

Generation X: Generation X'ers tend to be more self-confident. You will find them wanting to negotiate. There is more focus on "green" products and making the world a better place. X'ers don't just expect honesty—they demand it. This group freely employs and enjoys technology. They are much more deliberate in their spending.

Tips for dealing with Generation X'ers:

- Get to the point in conversations. Avoid hyperbole and cliché, as they can be irritants.
- Understand they expect you to use technology to communicate effectively.
- Recognize that it may take time to earn the respect of a Generation X worker—it is seldom given as a gift.
- Provide only the details requested, as they feel quite capable of working through issues.

Millennials: This generation lives technology. They are highly optimistic, and often believe they can do anything. Spending their parents' money is acceptable, and they often influence their parents' buying trends. Millennials typically work to live—don't live to work. They are into experiences and authenticity. They know "real" when they see it. It is important to talk *with* millennials, not *to* them.

Tips for working with millennials:

- Show knowledge and empowerment to provide what is needed. Millennials are reassured by the presence of an authority figure.
- Be prepared for high expectations when working through issues. They want authenticity in people and products and feel comfortable challenging others.
- Partner with them when working through issues.

Generation Z: This generation has been shaped by a post-9/11 world and our war on terror. They tend to be conservative with their money. The oldest Z's are working and saving what they earn. They do not like debt. When faced with a problem, they take action. These individuals are the "now" (Google) generation and expect information immediately through their handheld devices. Slow and cumbersome processes can be irritants. For the customer service professional, this means using the media (and speed) they use and trust.

Tips for working with Generation Z:

- Be prepared for many questions and challenges in working through issues.
- Recognize that Generation Z'ers may not be equipped with complete or accurate information. As my doctor says, he has a hard time competing with "Dr. Google." Remember, the customer is not always right.
- Discover ways to make your interactions and processes as smooth and timely as possible.

Conclusion

In this chapter we addressed the elements that influence behavior. Obviously, customers and their needs are not one-size-fits-all. For the customer service professional to more effectively serve, understanding the drivers behind their customers' (and their own) behavior is critical.

Chapter Review Questions

1. People might be thought of as icebergs because:
    a. They can appear very cold to others.
    b. Most of what drives a person's behavior is not easily visible.
    c. They tend to float in water.
    d. They are guided by external forces.

2. The "public us" is defined as:
    a. Appearance and values
    b. Behavior and needs
    c. Appearance and personality
    d. Appearance and behaviors

3. Sarah is very friendly in her customer interactions; however, in their absence she speaks negatively of them. Reflecting on the iceberg model, what is likely occurring?
    a. Sarah is manipulating her behaviors in the presence of customers.
    b. Sarah does not possess an attitude of service.
    c. Sarah may have a high need for power.
    d. All of the above.

4. Innate needs are learned.
    a. True
    b. False

5. Which of the following is not considered an acquired need?
    a. Need for affiliation
    b. Need for esteem
    c. Need for achievement
    d. Need for nutrition

6. Latoya volunteers at the local soup kitchen because it makes her feel good to help. Which of the following needs describes the source of her behavior?
   a. Need for social engagement
   b. Need for esteem
   c. Need for achievement
   d. Need for recognition

7. Which personality trait might best fit a customer who is very loud and boisterous?
   a. Feeler
   b. Extravert
   c. Perceiver
   d. Introvert

8. When considering personalities, Thinkers tend to be influenced by logic, while Feelers tend to be influenced by emotion.
   a. True
   b. False

9. When a service breakdown occurs, which customer personality preference is more apt to lead to outside-the-box solutions?
   a. Extraversion
   b. Intuition
   c. Perceiving
   d. Judging

10. Which of the following is most accurate regarding personal values?
    a. Principled behavior is grounded in strong values.
    b. Customers are not likely to be concerned about a company's values.
    c. It is important to do what is right if someone might observe you.
    d. Adherence to one's values must be situationally considered.

11. Recognizing that people—employees and customers—have vastly different experiential circumstances is cause to "customize" our approach to individuals.
    a. True
    b. False

12. Generational studies suggest people can be placed into what five categories?
    a. Traditionals/Matures, Post-War Boomers, Generation W, Millennials and Generation Z
    b. Veterans, Baby Boomers, Generation X, Millennials and Generation Y
    c. Traditionals/Matures, Baby Boomers, Generation X, Millennials and Generation Z
    d. Matures, Boomers, Generation X, Realists and Generation Y

13. It is critical for the customer service professional to interact with each generation in the same manner.
    a. True
    b. False

14. Which of the following is the most accurate?
    a. Millennials have a "take-it-or-leave-it" attitude toward technology.
    b. Realists tend to have a better understanding of life events in general.
    c. Generation X'ers enjoy hyperbole and cliché.
    d. Matures believe that integrity is an absolute.

15. Bottom line, we can change our attitudes given the knowledge and motivation to do so.
    a. True
    b. False

CHAPTER 3

Planning

We Plan a Lot

Individuals and organizations make many plans, whether instinctively or deliberately. In our personal lives, it might be planning for a summer vacation, remodeling the bathroom or just going out to dinner Saturday night. In an organization, we might plan for a new building, adding employees or preparing the annual budget. Simply defined,

> **Planning is the process of setting goals, developing strategies and outlining tasks and schedules to accomplish the goals.**

If you fail to plan, you are planning to fail.
—Benjamin Franklin

Planning is an essential component of everyday life—whether short-term, like going to dinner on Saturday, or long-term, like building a new facility. All plans require thought about some objective we want to achieve. When we fail to plan, we may find ourselves at the mercy of day-to-day circumstances. When we are planful, we understand our objective, what resources are available and what obstacles we might encounter, and we develop strategies to mitigate those obstacles. When we plan, we have greater control over resources and our outcomes.

> **There is no shallow end in the planning pool.**
> —C. WILLIAM CRUTCHER

Planning cannot be a sometimes, "when it is convenient" activity. It must be woven into the fabric of daily activities. Planning guides what we do every day.

We have seen organizations that energetically develop a strategic plan. Early on, they prioritize planning time and seem to enjoy the initial steps—creating a mission, vision and values. Unfortunately, because effective planning requires a dedicated ongoing effort, some organizations begin to find reasons to discontinue the process, and thus lose the benefits of a well-constructed plan.

WHY WE PLAN

While we may intuitively understand the need to plan, research indicates we typically engage in planning for three primary reasons.

1. *Provides direction:* There is an old saying: "If you don't know where you are going, how will you know when you get there?" We may chuckle when we hear this, but the message is important. The planning process clarifies for us and others what objectives we want to achieve—where we are going—and allows us to celebrate a successful arrival. A well-developed, well-articulated plan contributes to both individual and organizational success.

2. *Minimizes waste and redundancy:* When we fail to adequately plan, we may find ourselves engaging in superfluous re-work, or in the case of our customers, in excessive recovery efforts. Planning allows us to better access our resources and deploy them for maximum effectiveness. For example, employees who have clearly defined job descriptions, relevant annual goals and an evaluation process accomplish much more

than employees who do not. In the words of Stephen Covey, we are most effective when we "begin with the end in mind."

3. *Helps you get to YOUR destination:* Through effective planning, we are far more likely to accomplish our goals. Most of us have had work-days where we didn't have an objective defining what we wanted to accomplish that day. We worked hard and at quitting time, we were tired. Reflecting back, we recognized that while we were busy, the day controlled us, versus us controlling the day. When we have meaningful plans in place, we are better equipped to manage obstacles that could derail our day and keep us from moving toward our desired end state.

Organizations that plan regularly and consistently tend to be more successful than those that do not. Likewise, individuals who plan regularly and consistently tend to reach higher levels of personal success. In essence, if we plan to do better, we often, in fact, do better!

If we have not been engaging in global planning, we might find committing time to periodical planning difficult, because we haven't developed the habit. However, the quality of your planning is more important than the quantity of your planning. A few well-developed plans will provide greater personal and organizational returns than numerous poorly developed plans.

If we plan, will we always be successful? The simple answer is no. However, research suggests that if we practice appropriate, meaningful planning, failure is more likely to be the result of environmental constraints—e.g., interest rates, material shortages, financial downturn—than the quality of our plans. We can mitigate these constraints by monitoring our external environment—keeping an eye on circumstances outside our control and doing our best to anticipate how they will impact our plans.

Organizational Planning

SUCCESSFUL PEOPLE AND ORGANIZATIONS EXPECTED TO BE

It should now be evident that successful individuals and organizations were not just lucky. They achieved because they planned to achieve. Not every plan is successful, but as we just discussed, success is more probable for the planful. This is equally true for the customer service professional, especially when our daily effort is tied to a clearly defined and well-articulated strategic plan.

Let's explore the components of a complete end-to-end strategic plan. As we do, relate both your personal and your organization's planning efforts to the structure discussed. The complete planning process can sometimes sound foreign and feel a bit overwhelming, but breaking it up into individual components reveals its logic and illuminates its inherent value.

STRATEGIC PLANNING MATRIX

From a high-level view, the plan contains two primary elements: strategic components and tactical or operations components. Different organizations may use various terms when discussing these components, and that is acceptable. Most important is that the plan is well articulated and understood by all employees.

Strategic Components

- **Core Organizational Values:** These values or value statements reflect the organization's operating philosophy. They may be stated as single words, such as "Honesty," "Integrity" or "Respect," or as phrases or statements such as "We will do whatever it takes to satisfy our customers."

The most effective organizational values are developed with input from all employee levels. There is an old saying that goes, "No one washes a rental car!" If you want employees to own and live these values, they need to be part of the development process. The larger

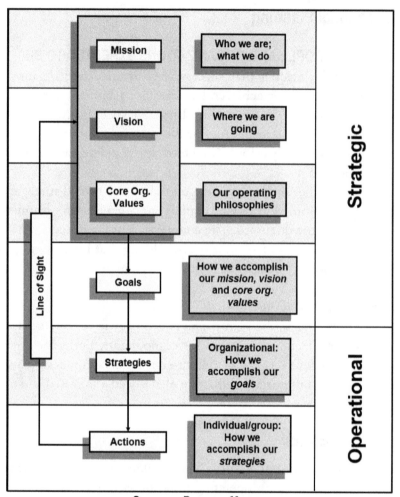

STRATEGIC PLANNING MATRIX

the organization, the greater the struggle to include all employees in this process. Multilevel, cross-functional focus groups may be the solution. Once the values have been developed, share them in employee meetings and provide an opportunity for feedback. This will create the necessary ownership.

- **Mission:** An organizational mission statement describes "who we are" and "what we do." This component of the strategic plan is typically developed by the organization's executive or leadership team. Smaller organizations may include other levels of representation.

  Mission statements can often be found on company websites. For example, CVS Corporation's mission statement, "We will be the easiest pharmacy retailer for customers to use," is brief and to the point. It tells us who they are and what they do: a pharmacy that makes it simple for people to shop at. Mission statements that are succinct and memorable help employees relate how their particular role supports its achievement. It is important that mission statements be worded in the "attained state." Words such as "strive to" or "we attempt" should be avoided. If we were to make a single suggestion to CVS, it would be to replace the words "will be" with "are," leaving no room for less than being the easiest pharmacy to use.

  Organizations often include *how* they are going to achieve their mission within the statement, which can make it excessively long and difficult, if not impossible, for employees to remember. Instead, the tactical or operational components of the plan will effectively address the "how to" portion of the mission statement. Remember, an effective mission statement is one that all employees can easily remember, understand and live.

- **Vision:** An organizational vision statement identifies where the organization is going. As with the mission statement, this component of the strategic plan is typically developed by the executive or leadership team. Again, like the mission statement, it should be succinct and memorable. A transit company we were working with developed the vision statement "A transit-reliant community." This organization recognized that bus ridership was well below what it could and should be. They understood that if a reasonable portion of the community began using the bus system, they would grow to prefer it and integrate it into their daily lives, becoming "transit-reliant." Every employee understood what this meant and was able to incorporate it into their daily work efforts.

An effective vision statement should be written in the future, describing an unattained state—one that has not yet been achieved. As the organization achieves or nears this desired state, the vision should be updated.

- **Strategic/Organizational Goals**
  Once again, the terms you select for this portion of the plan are not important, though agreeing on what they mean is. Strategic or organizational goals indicate how an organization accomplishes its mission, vision and values. These high-level goals are essentially "distilled" from the mission, vision and values statements. Most organizations will develop only a few strategic goals encompassing key areas of products and services, financial stability, community impact and employees. Following are examples of strategic goals:

  ◊ Products/services: To be the lowest-cost provider of Internet service in the country.
  ◊ Financial stability: To maintain the dominant market share in the areas we serve.
  ◊ Community: To support local charities in our market areas.
  ◊ Employees: To attract and retain the most talented individuals in our field.

  It should be apparent that multiple strategies are required to accomplish each of these high-level goals. Thus the strategic planning process can be thought of as a "distillation process"—each subsequent set supports the step above it.

Tactical/Operational Components

- **Strategies:** Some organizations may refer to strategies as "operational goals" or simply "goals." The key is that they determine how the strategic/organizational goals will be accomplished. They are typically organizational in nature—i.e., more than one individual is accountable for their achievement. To better understand, let's refer back to our "Employees" strategic goal above, "To attract the most talented individuals in our field." One strategy to ensure this goal is accomplished might be "Offer competitive wages to all employees." While this is an important strategy, there are of course many others to attract and retain the most talented individuals. These could include vacation time or tuition assistance programs.

• **Objectives:** Also known as "activities" or "tactics" by some organizations, objectives are quite specific or finite in the actions they define. They represent how strategies are accomplished and are individual in nature. To be most effective, objectives identify one person as "owner" for ensuring their completion. That is not to say that others are not engaged in the objective's activities; however, the owner would be accountable for its ultimate achievement (or failure).

Let's continue our example from above. If our strategy is "Offer competitive wages to all employees," a reasonable objective might be "Complete a comparative salary analysis annually to benchmark similar industry jobs." The organization would then have a basis for recognizing what competitive pay ranges actually look like.

"Line of Sight"

In planning terminology, "line of sight" refers to the premise that all objectives—or work activities—should be planful and contribute to the organization achieving its mission, vision and values. This is often called goal-directed work behavior. What creates "line of sight" is the overall distillation (strategic planning) process that leads to the development of individual objectives. So when employees collectively satisfy objectives linked to the mission, vision and values, the organization enjoys high levels of success.

NO OR INCOMPLETE PLANNING

The reality is that only the most effective organizations "stay in the pool" and plan on a regular and consistent basis. Hopefully, your company is one that does. However, even in the absence of a comprehensive, enterprise-wide practice, anyone can take measures to be more planful. As indicated earlier, a little good planning is preferable to a lot of poor planning.

- **For the Organizational Leader**
  If you represent the entire organization, your challenge has been laid out for you. Begin the process and commit to staying engaged on a regular, ongoing basis. Follow the steps just described and you will enjoy a greater likelihood of success.

- **For the Department or Group Leader**
  With or without a large organizational plan, consider developing your group or department's mission, vision and values. For example, if you are a customer call center, what would your mission be? Who are you and what do you do? What about your vision? Where are you going as a call center? Are you aiming to be the best in the nation in overall customer satisfaction? That is a tall order but one you certainly could explore. What about your values? Are you a customer-centric call center—one that recognizes that excellence in customer service is a planful concept? Imagine the excitement and commitment of your employees working to develop this plan. Follow the process above and each customer service representative's daily work effort will feed directly into your mission, vision and values. Your employees will also willingly "own" the group or department's mission, vision and values.

- **For the Individual**
  While the organization or your department might now be planful, there is plenty of opportunity for you to be as well. Use your knowledge and experience to establish objectives that will focus your work activities on positive individual and organizational outcomes. It is helpful to think about the stakeholders who influence what you do. These may include:
  - ◊ Customers
  - ◊ Employees
  - ◊ Community

◊ Government
◊ Competitors
◊ Suppliers

A simple way to evaluate your objectives is the "3-M" test:

◊ Meaningful: Will it contribute in a significant manner to your overall expected accomplishments?
◊ Makeable: Is it something you can reasonably achieve?
◊ Measurable: Can success be measured in absolute terms and not through abstractions such as better, larger, more, etc.?

You need not develop objectives regarding each of your stakeholders, only those most critical to your personal mission. For example, if your work is heavily regulated, you may develop an objective to monitor federal regulation updates for your industry.

There are complex goal-development templates. It doesn't matter which form is used as long as it is simple and easily understood. When the process becomes too difficult or burdensome, it becomes your master instead of your servant and it will eventually be abandoned.

In summary, planning is one of the most important contributors to individual and organizational success. The act of planning is the difference between winning and losing. It is often the key to attracting and retaining a loyal customer base.

Chapter Review Questions

1. Planning involves which of the following?
   a. Setting goals
   b. Developing strategies
   c. Outlining tasks and schedules
   d. All of the above

2. Effective planning can only be done when there is available time.
   a. True
   b. False

3. Which of the following is not a primary reason for planning?
   a. Providing direction
   b. Gaining community involvement
   c. Minimizing waste and redundancy
   d. Assuring the right goals are accomplished

4. The quality of planning is more important than the quantity of planning.
   a. True
   b. False

5. Which of the following describes who the organization is and what it does?
   a. Vision
   b. Core organizational values
   c. Mission
   d. Strategies

6. The end-to-end strategic plan consists of what two primary component groups?
    a. Operational and strategic
    b. Goals and objectives
    c. Operational and tactical
    d. Strategies and objectives

7. A mission statement should be worded in the "attained" state. Which of the following is an acceptable opening for a valid mission statement?
    a. "We hope to be . . ."
    b. "We strive to be . . ."
    c. "We are the . . ."
    d. "We want to be . . ."

8. Organizations should develop only a few strategic goals.
    a. True
    b. False

9. "Line of sight" in strategic planning:
    a. Refers to the premise that all work activities should contribute to the achievement of an organization's mission, vision and values
    b. Identifies how much of the organization is within your purview
    c. Indicates the number of employees in an individual's chain of command
    d. Determines the volume of operational goals within a particular work unit

10. Which of the following could be considered an organization's stakeholders?
    a. Customers
    b. Employees
    c. Community
    d. Government
    e. All of the above

11. Which of the following is not part of the "3-M" goal-setting test?
    a. It is meaningful.
    b. It is malleable.
    c. It is makeable.
    d. It is measurable.

12. "There is no shallow end in the planning pool" refers to what?
    a. Planning must be something that is done on a continual basis.
    b. Planning cannot be done by an individual.
    c. Planning should only be attempted by seasoned professionals.
    d. An organization can "drown" through excessive planning.

13. Choosing where to go for dinner on the weekend is engaging in planning.
    a. True
    b. False

14. What can be said about an organization that engages in ongoing planning?
    a. Net income is maintained.
    b. The cost of planning can often outweigh the benefits.
    c. Overall, it will be more successful than organizations that do not engage in planning.
    d. Employee productivity may diminish due to the time required to plan.

15. An organization's core operating values are best developed by senior management.
    a. True
    b. False

CHAPTER 4

Effective Communication Strategies

Why We Communicate

Everyone learns at a very early age to communicate. We do this for a variety of reasons. Some are quite obvious—to seek food, guidance, support, etc.—and others are not. Research suggests we communicate primarily for the following reasons:

1. *Inform or Share:* We relay information to others to advise them of something. It could be a child indicating they have play rehearsal tomorrow or a company advisory that the computer system will be down on Friday for maintenance. Regardless of the audience or the content, communication is designed to share information with others.

2. *Direct:* In this case, we provide instructions to others indicating how to achieve something. It could be a phone representative explaining how to use a particular application, or a customer service professional advising a customer on how to complete an online form. These are often referred to as "teaching" and "learning" situations.

3. *Seek Guidance or Clarity:* Your supervisor may have asked you to complete a task and you are unclear on the specific deliverables. In this instance, you contact your supervisor to gain clarity on what is expected from you. People seek guidance often and in many ways, from asking a pedestrian for directions to a restaurant, to hiring a personal coach. All such communications are designed to provide clarity.

4. *Build Relationships:* As we discussed in Chapter 2, what drives each of us is both similar and unique. To learn more about others—especially customers—we communicate in a manner conducive to understanding different paradigms, or drivers of behavior. This is how we discover our similarities, differences and, in the case of customers, how to better serve.

5. *Admonish or Correct:* Sometimes, despite best intentions and well-developed plans, others do not behave as expected. Here, we communicate both to attempt to fix the situation and to convey the consequences of similar future actions. Parents do this with their children when they declare a "time-out." In business, admonishment might take the form of a stern lecture or disciplinary letter, accompanied by the real or potential consequences of such action.

So which of these five purposes applies to more than 50 percent of human communication? We might immediately think that number 1—to share information—is the obvious answer. In reality, we spend the majority of human communication on number 4—building relationships. Though it might come in smaller, briefer segments, learning about others and sharing about ourselves is at the heart of most conversations. From a customer service perspective, this means learning about our customer so we can serve them better.

INTERPERSONAL COMMUNICATION PROCESS

What are the mechanics of communication? Diagram 4-1 illustrates the process we follow in communicating with one another.

- *Sender:* Someone initiates the communication. The sender is the person who begins the process, and they determine who will be the receiver(s) of the communication.

- *Encode:* The sender converts their thoughts into a message, conveying what the sender wants to communicate. This could be oral, written or expressive, such as a picture.

- *Medium:* The sender chooses what modality to employ to transmit the message to the receiver(s). If the message is in oral form, the medium could be electronic—e.g., a phone call—or a face-to-face conversation. If the message is in written form, it could be delivered in hardcopy or electronically, such as an email.

- *Receiver:* This is the intended recipient of the sender's message. There may be multiple receivers, dependent upon the nature of the message.

- *Decode:* Once the receiver has obtained the message, they must now decode or interpret it. In the diagram, the sender intended to transmit the message "A+B"; however, the receiver interpreted the message as "B+C." Unfortunately, our communications are too often misinterpreted in this stage.

- *Feedback:* Effective communication provides a channel for the recipient to seek any desired clarity on the message. This channel is often vague with broadcast (large group) announcements. The feedback link is necessary to ensure expectations are understood and managed.

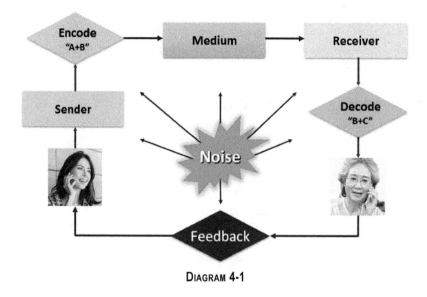

DIAGRAM 4-1

- *Noise:* This is the reason that intended messages are not identical to received messages. We will elaborate on "noise" in the following pages.

Why Communication Breaks Down

As we just discussed, recipients do not always get the intended message. This is due to several factors:

- *Too many links in the chain:* If you have ever played the game where you whisper a message into someone's ear and they whisper it to the next person and so forth until the last person announces the message they heard, you know the final version of the original message is never the same, and often, hilariously inaccurate. This is because each person receives only part of the message, filling in the rest with their imagination. In the business world, as communiqués are passed down in different forms, the original message becomes muddled, if not lost entirely.

- *Undefined expectations:* In this case, the recipient lacks complete information to deliver what the requestor expected. For example, you are facilitating a workshop on customer service. You take your PowerPoint file on a flash drive to the copy shop. You tell the print department employee you need 30 copies of the handouts, collated and stapled. When you return to pick up your copies, you discover each slide was printed on a separate page, single sided and stapled at the top middle. What you actually wanted was two slides per page, double sided and stapled in the upper left corner. Did you get your handouts? Yes, but not the handouts you wanted. Anytime we receive a request, it serves us well to ensure that the specifics are understood. When we are the requestor, it is important to consider what the recipient needs to know to complete the task as expected.

- *Failure to consider differences in communication skills:* We all have varying skills in many disciplines. Communication is no different. This is especially true when it comes to modern technology. Reflecting back on generational differences discussed in Chapter 2, we shouldn't be surprised to learn that many traditionals/matures may be challenged in using current electronic devices and applications. And younger people—though skillful with modern technology—may lack an understanding of business writing. For the customer service professional, it is imperative that communication strategies fit the intended audience.

- *Noise:* As Diagram 4-1 shows, "noise" is a pervasive phenomenon that often derails effective communication. Let's explore "noise" in more detail.

NOISE: BARRIERS TO EFFECTIVE COMMUNICATION

When we think of "noise," "sound" immediately comes to mind. Let's dig deeper into the various forms of "noise" and their impact on effective communication.

- *Sound:* The typical "noise" we tend to think of. Most of us have fallen victim to the sounds of a crowded restaurant, heavy traffic, etc. In these situations, it can be a struggle to hear and be heard. Listening is strained, as background sounds interfere with receiving the correct message. These interferences require that we adjust our communication approach to ensure the intended message is received.

- *Filtering:* When employees are reluctant to share negative news with their boss, they might filter the message by modifying it to more favorable terms so it is better accepted. This happens most often in poor supervisor-subordinate relationships. When it comes to the customer, truthfulness is an absolute. If a customer suspects, or worse, discovers, the customer service professional has not been fully honest, that relationship is likely doomed. When the relationship is positive, however, the customer is apt to tolerate occasional setbacks and work with the customer service professional to find resolutions.

- *Selective Reception:* In this case, the recipient hears what they want to hear, not the entire message communicated. Consider customer surveys as an example. We commonly focus only on the negative—

hopefully constructive—comments shared. While such feedback can represent opportunities to improve the business, it should be balanced with the positive comments as well. A more serious problem with selective reception is focusing only on the favorable and not exploring how to effectively employ the critical feedback.

- *Emotions:* When individuals are emotional, they do not hear all that is being said. The more emotional the person, the worse their position to work through an issue. We will discuss this topic further when we explore effective listening strategies.

- *Information Overload:* Today, information comes at us quickly, from multiple sources, nonstop. Walk into any business meeting and you will likely see the "participants" on their phones, emailing or texting others outside the meeting. When asked, they often explain that "multitasking" is integral to their job. In reality, no one is wired to multitask. Our brains allow us to perform one high-level cognitive task at a time. So, when we are in a meeting and start looking at our phone, we are no longer engaged in that meeting. Neither of those interactions gets 100 percent of our attention. We are seeing more and more automobile accidents as a result of drivers using their phones. Many of us suffer from CPA—Continuous Partial Attention—which occurs when we try to engage in multiple high-level cognitive tasks simultaneously. From a customer service perspective, it is critical to be 100 percent engaged with the customer. Otherwise, they feel unworthy of your time and will "vote with their feet." The key is to learn to manage multiple priorities and avoid fruitless attempts at multitasking.

- *Defensiveness:* When confronted with a problem, we sometimes fixate on proving we are right rather than seeking an effective resolution. When we do this, we ignore or reject opportunities to fix the situation. As a customer service professional, your job is to facilitate a balanced solution—not lay blame.

- *Language/Jargon:* Here, we are not talking about a foreign language. We are referring to the use of company-specific terms. Every business has its own short forms, abbreviations or acronyms for internal efficiency. But your customers must always fully understand what you are communicating. Using jargon may be viewed as intentionally confusing or intimidating the customer and is a sure way to lose business.

- *Culture:* Individuals from other countries or even regions of the United States have cultural differences. The role of the customer service professional is to recognize these differences and adjust communication accordingly. Customer service is not a one-size-fits-all proposition. Knowing and responding to your customers' cultural expectations is key to retaining them.

Communication Styles

Because we are diverse, we employ different communication styles, including passive, aggressive, assertive and the all-too-familiar passive-aggressive approaches.

- *Passive:* We allow things to happen or accept what other people do.
- *Aggressive:* We are ready and willing to fight, argue or use other forceful methods to succeed.
- *Assertive:* We are self-confident, decisive, firm and emphatic.

The style we use typically depends upon the situation—who we are communicating with and how much power we sense we have—and the importance of the outcome to us. The more powerful we feel and the more important the issue, the greater the likelihood that we become aggressive in the communication. The less our perceived power and the importance of the issue, the more likely we are to be passive.

Ideally, all individuals should adopt an assertive approach to interpersonal communication, as it is the style most likely to lead to positive outcomes for all concerned. Here is a more complete functional definition:

Assertiveness is the ability to communicate clearly, succinctly and persuasively what you want or need from another person or persons in a manner that produces a two-way, respectful conversation.

Assertive in-person communication is evidenced by the characteristics below. As you review the list, conduct a high-level evaluation of how you approach interpersonal communication. Some of these characteristics will become clearer by the end of this chapter.

- *Verbal:* Wants and feelings are clearly articulated. Assertive language leaves no doubt regarding the speaker's expectations. (Note: Since assertive communication is always respectful, this approach is always clear but never "brutal.")

- *Nonverbal:* Attentive, active listening is exhibited.

- *Voice:* Speech is well modulated—firm, but warm. The volume is not too loud or soft, but easy to listen to.

- *Eyes:* Eyes are open with good—not uncomfortable—eye contact. Glancing away occasionally is preferred.

- *Stance:* Posture is balanced and relaxed. Personal space is acknowledged and respected.

- *Hands:* Relaxed movement is maintained. We all know people who talk with their hands. Assertive communication involves minimal hand motion and a neutral position. We will explore nonverbal communication in greater depth below.

Each of us should strive to adopt an assertive communication style. When we are aggressive, we do not "hear" the other person and appear as dominating the conversation, which leads to lost customers. When we are passive, we are not truly "heard" by others and therefore provide little value. When we are passive-aggressive, we are not trustworthy and people will avoid us. As a customer service professional, the only clear style for maintaining positive customer service relationships is an assertive one.

Communication Types or Mediums

In addition to styles, there are also several communication types or mediums—the method and manner in which we choose to communicate. Our goal must be to maximize the *effectiveness* of our communication, regardless of the type of communication medium chosen.

We can define communication *effectiveness* as the extent to which the selected medium of communication allows both the sender and the receiver of the information to reach a common understanding of the intended message. Simply stated, was the intended message accurately received by the intended receiver?

Diagram 4-2 depicts the level of effectiveness of various communications mediums.

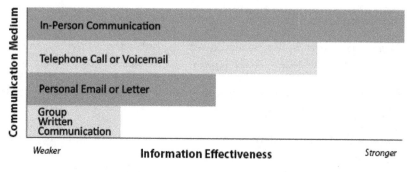

DIAGRAM 4-2

A group written communication might take the form of a company bulletin or blast email to notify employees of an upcoming insurance enrollment period. Because this message is for numerous employees, it cannot contain personalized information. Additionally, because it only contains written words (or graphics), it lacks voice intonation and nonverbals.

In the personal email or letter, information can be geared to a specific individual. Both are "delivered" to a specific recipient. Again, because we lack voice intonation and nonverbals, the effectiveness is on the weaker end. In both written types, we must count on the words being construed literally. "Great" must mean exactly that, and not the disgusted sentiment which can't be heard in writing.

Even stronger information effectiveness is found in a telephone call or voicemail. In these situations, we have added voice intonation to the message, enhancing its effectiveness and subsequent understanding. The intended meaning of "great" can be more clearly understood.

The highest level of information effectiveness emerges with in-person communication. Here, we have the words, voice intonation and nonverbals, which, combined, maximize the likelihood of receiving the intended message. In today's business environment, it is quite common to use applications such as Skype for our communication purposes. Please note that while these applications do provide a great deal of the "in-person" communication dynamics, the quality of technology employed, combined with the visual "cropping" of individuals, may reduce overall communication effectiveness.

When dealing with customers, it is always best to use the strongest, most effective form of communication—especially when complicated issues such as service breakdowns arise. The sterility of back-and-forth emails does not help recovery efforts.

The work of Albert Mehrabian, a pioneer of communications since the 1960s and professor emeritus at UCLA, confirmed the significance of information effectiveness. Studying thousands of in-person conversations, Mehrabian discovered that the relative importance to the listener of a message's elements is as follows:

- Words used: 7%
- Vocal tone: 38%
- Nonverbals: 55%

To ensure the message intended is the message received, we should strive to make communication in-person when possible. Second best is by telephone. Writing should be our last choice, especially for sensitive and timely issues.

Nonverbal Communication

As we just discussed, nonverbal messages are an integral component of communication. Nonverbals reinforce and define the spoken word. They may even replace the spoken word. Nonverbals also provide feedback and assurance that we are listening. Simply defined,

> **Nonverbal communication is the movements, gestures and other physical signals that clarify or confuse the meaning of the verbal communication.**

Nonverbals can be confusing if they do not support the other parts of the communication. Take for example a boy asking his father if he can go down the street to play with a friend. The father replies "yes," while shaking his head "no." This was likely done in jest; however, it exemplifies that nonverbals can detract from the intended message. We might refer to nonverbals as either "contributors"—supporting the intended message—or "detractors"—inhibiting receipt of the intended message. Let's consider examples of each:

Detractors
- Crossed arms
- No or little eye contact
- Looking at watch
- Looking at phone
- Pointing finger
- Hands on hips
- Head shaking

When we exhibit one or more of these nonverbals, it detracts from the listener's ability to stay focused on the message. Instead, we find ourselves wondering why the listener appears to not be listening or liking the message. This can derail our train of thought and the delivery of our intended message.

Other nonverbals can enhance the interaction and contribute to a better understanding of the intended message. Consider the following examples:

Contributors
- Relaxed posture
- Nodding with acknowledgement
- Good eye contact
- Intent focus
- Smiling
- Look of concern (as appropriate)

It should be noted that "nodding with acknowledgment" is different than "nodding in agreement." When the listener is nodding their head, they are typically indicating they hear and understand what the speaker is saying. It is important that the speaker not misinterpret this as agreement with the message. Clarification in this instance is appropriate.

As we just noted, nonverbals are eight times more powerful than the words we speak. The customer service professional must appreciate that what the customer sees is far more important than what they hear. Saying the word "yes" but nonverbally indicating "no" is unsettling to customers and may cause them to seek service elsewhere.

Voice Inflection

The intonation in our voice can also reinforce or modify the spoken word. How often do we hear the word "great" when the speaker means just the opposite? That is the power of voice inflection. In the written word, "great" has to be used literally—meaning boundless, unlimited or wonderful, and nothing else. The reader only sees the word and does not hear the intended inflection that would cause it to mean lowly or awful.

In phone calls and in-person interactions, intonation facilitates understanding of the message. It is important to recognize, though, that not all phones and devices transmit with equal clarity. Using your words literally is a safe bet on the phone. If something is awful—say it is awful.

Rate of Speech

All of us have listened to someone speak overly slowly. Or at the other extreme, you're probably familiar with those disclaimers at the end of television commercials that are so fast you strain to understand.

The rate at which we speak is an important part of communication. Research suggests that the average person comprehends best at a rate of 140–150 words per minute. This allows us to hear all the words, pick up on any voice inflection and then process the communication. Find a paragraph—or create one—that is 140–150 words in length. Time yourself reading the paragraph until you are able to complete it in approximately one minute. It is common to feel that this rate seems slow, but it is the optimal one for the listener. This is a good exercise if you speak with customers on the phone. Speaking at 140–150 words per minute will make you a much more effective and better-received communicator.

Listening

In face-to-face communication, how much time do you spend speaking versus listening? If we are honest with ourselves, most of us find we speak more than we listen. We learn when we are listening, not when we are speaking. Personal and professional growth demands we be effective listeners. It is also an integral part of assertive communication.

Here are some interesting statistics. The average person speaks at a rate of 125–150 words per minute. We comprehend up to 600 words per minute, and we think at 1,000–3,000 words per minute. Because words are spoken to us much slower than we can think, we often lose concentration and may not fully hear the speaker. Thus, it is critical that we engage in effective or active listening.

What constitutes effective listening?

- Maintaining good eye contact

- Paraphrasing—"speaking back"—as appropriate, to confirm what the speaker is saying
- Using nonverbal affirmations—e.g., head nod, smile
- Avoiding distracting mannerisms—e.g., looking at your watch
- Asking appropriate questions to seek clarity
- Balancing talking and listening
- Summarizing at the end of the other person's statement

LISTEN MORE THAN YOU SPEAK

Research on face-to-face and telephonic communications in U.S. culture suggests that we spend most of our time speaking or preparing to speak. As a result, people do not feel fully heard. For a customer service professional, a useful mantra might be, "Listen more than I speak." Listening sets you up to learn from the customer and better positions you to serve.

The highest form of listening is empathic—listening beyond the words, intonation and nonverbals to recognize the speaker's emotion.

Empathic listening is listening and responding in such a manner as to virtually project yourself into the emotions of the other person.

More simply stated,

Empathic listening is listening for feelings with your eyes.

Recall that emotion is a type of "noise" and interferes with transmission of the intended message. Take, for example, an angry customer. As the customer service professional, you might attempt to provide a solution to satisfy what you perceive as the customer's needs. But the customer is not willing to accept it. Instead, they continue to speak loudly and emotionally.

Until you acknowledge the customer's condition—that they are upset—they will not be ready to accept any solution. You might say, "I can see you are upset, and I would be too in this situation." And it might take

67

several moments of acknowledging their emotion to reach a point where you can provide an acceptable solution. Remember, the customer is looking for recognition and validation of their current state. Once they are satisfied that you can relate to their emotion, you will be able to proceed with assistance.

So, why should we engage in empathic listening? There are several reasons:

- It reduces tensions—offering solutions before the customer is ready only heightens the tension.
- It provides for a release of emotions.
- It allows for a sharing of the real issues.
- It provides a safe zone—so the other person feels comfortable sharing the "why" of their emotion.
- It builds trust and respect—you are seen as an understanding partner.

This said, make sure you understand your company's policy regarding how to respond if the dialogue becomes abusive.

As we have discussed, listening is far more than just hearing. Here is a summary of effective listening habits:

- Listen attentively—use positive nonverbals.
- Do not interrupt unnecessarily—listen more than you speak.
- Respond versus react—it is more thoughtful, appreciated and productive.
- Clarify as necessary—use caution not to probe unnecessarily.
- Listen nonjudgmentally.
- Offer input as appropriate.
- Be empathic—recognize the emotion.

It takes a wide variety of skills to be an effective customer service professional. At the top is the ability to communicate effectively. It permeates all we do and largely determines our success—or failure. Communication skills should therefore be learned and mastered by all customer service professionals.

Chapter Review Questions

1. Which of the following are reasons we communicate?
    a. Inform or share
    b. Direct others
    c. Seek guidance or clarity
    d. Build relationships
    e. All of the above

2. Which of the following is not a reason communication breaks down?
    a. Defined expectations
    b. Too many links in the chain
    c. Differences in communication skills
    d. Noise

3. Steven only tells his customers what he thinks they want to hear. This is an example of what kind of communication "noise"?
    a. Actual sounds
    b. Filtering
    c. Emotion
    d. Information overload

4. Ideally, we should strive for which communication style?
    a. Passive
    b. Aggressive
    c. Passive-aggressive
    d. Assertive

5. Brutal honesty should always be employed in in-person communication.
    a. True
    b. False

6. Mary must communicate with an upset customer. Which communication medium should Mary use that will provide the greatest level of "information effectiveness"?
    a. Written group communication
    b. Personal email or letter
    c. In-person meeting
    d. Telephone call or voicemail

7. Which of the following did Albert Mehrabian's research find carried the most impact in in-person communication?
    a. Nonverbals
    b. Vocal tone
    c. Words used
    d. Attitude

8. Nonverbals only serve to clarify verbal communication.
    a. True
    b. False

9. Which of the following is a detractor from effective communication?
    a. Relaxed posture
    b. Looking at watch
    c. Good eye contact
    d. Smiling

10. Which rate of speaking is best for being readily understood?
    a. 300 words per minute
    b. 250 words per minute
    c. 60 words per minute
    d. 140–150 words per minute

11. Which of the following may lead to ineffective listening?
    a. Balancing talking and listening
    b. Using positive nonverbals
    c. Remaining silent
    d. Paraphrasing as appropriate

12. Which best describes U.S. culture when it comes to speaking and listening?
    a. The majority of people are excellent listeners.
    b. Most people are poor speakers.
    c. It is difficult to hear in crowded rooms.
    d. During conversations, most people are either speaking or preparing to speak.

13. We learn more about customers when we are:
    a. Speaking
    b. Listening

14. Simply stated, empathic listening is:
    a. Listening for feelings with your eyes
    b. Crying for someone
    c. Feeling sorry for a person
    d. Ignoring emotion to solve a problem

15. We spend more than 50 percent of human communication building relationships.
    a. True
    b. False

CHAPTER 5

Effective Teaming

We Are Not Alone

Rarely does anyone succeed without assistance from others, whether they be coworkers, colleagues, family, friends or strangers. Even the best and brightest do not work in a vacuum. In this chapter we explore aspects of working interdependently—"teaming"—and its impact on effective customer service.

WHY WE JOIN TEAMS

Most people belong to several groups or teams. (We will explore the difference momentarily.) Some join the local Rotary Club, others a church or a charity. While we may not consciously rationalize our motives, we are drawn to them for a variety of reasons. Some of the primary drivers include:

- *Security/Power:* Being part of a group or team reduces our insecurity of standing alone. We are able to better withstand threats from nonmembers. This is evidenced in protests or a group of parents confronting a local school board. We feel strength in numbers.

- *Status:* Some like to belong to a group or team that is viewed by outsiders as important or exclusive. They like the recognition. This is what might drive a person to become a member of "the" country club, or serve on a charity's board of directors with other high-status community members.

- *Self-Esteem:* We become a member of certain groups and teams to feel good about ourselves—to feel we are of value. This is a key driver for most charitable work. Volunteering at a food drive, for example, can be greatly satisfying.

- *Affiliation:* In this case, we want to fulfill a sense of belonging. Most individuals do not like the idea or feeling of being alone. Teams and groups can fill important social and personal needs.

- *Achievement:* Some tasks are impossible to achieve alone, and a pool of talent is necessary for success. Bringing together individuals with specific skills is common on more complex projects.

Considering these rationales, it is evident why teams are so popular and why we choose to join them. In the workplace, they meld complementary skills and typically achieve faster results than an individual alone. They facilitate employee participation in operational decision-making, which significantly boosts morale. Groups and teams also provide a social dimension and create a fun work environment. Hard work does not have to be dismal work.

GROUP VERSUS TEAM

So what is the difference between a group and a team? In practical terms,

A group is two or more people who come together for a common purpose.

The same could be said for a team, right? Let's look at an example. On Saturday, you and a friend go to the theater to see a popular new movie. There are over a hundred people there. Does this fit the above definition of a group? Yes, there are certainly more than two people and everyone came to see the same movie. But are they a team? Most of us would say no, and we would be correct. What is it, then, that differentiates a group from a team?

Imagine we are watching the local college basketball team in action. They are actually called a team. Is it because they all wear the same uniform? If that were the case, then we could put everyone at work into the same uniform and have a team. Do all sports teams really "team" effectively? We know the answer to that question is no.

In our years of work in the field of teaming, we have discovered the most significant difference between a group and a team is *commitment*. Groups become teams when the members are highly cohesive. It is almost a vow, a pledge to one another to support and defend each member and make the personal effort necessary to achieve the team's objective(s). That is why groups wearing the same uniform can fail, and teams with members from disparate backgrounds often succeed. As a customer service professional, ask yourself: "Are we collectively committed to one another and to the service of our customers?" Remember, your team members are also your customers.

The BIG "C" in Teaming Is Commitment!

THE ESSENTIALS OF EFFECTIVE TEAMING
While member commitment is at the foundation of successful teams, ongoing team effectiveness relies on other key elements as well. With the exception of commitment, the following are in no particular order and are equally important.

- *Commitment:* The cornerstone of teaming described above.

- *Principled Leadership:* Team members will follow someone who displays honesty, integrity and respect. Individuals who do not consistently behave as such cannot expect team loyalty. If a leader is not respectful and respectable, they will not, in turn, be respected. When we do not respect or trust a leader, we will not commit ourselves 100 percent, and both the leader and the team lose. Successful teams have leaders who live the organization's values every day.

- *Support and Recognition:* Here we refer to support and recognition from people external to the team. Imagine, for example, you are part of a team tasked with developing and implementing process improvements that will streamline the customer experience. Your team comes up with excellent ideas, but they are constantly rejected or ignored by management. Before long, motivation dwindles and the team becomes inconsequential as members shift their attention and energy to other activities. Teams with leadership as cheerleaders are motivated and will make the effort to succeed.

- *Member Competency:* Motivation and willingness to engage in goal-directed work isn't sufficient for team effectiveness. Individual members must have the necessary skills and capacity to fulfill their role. In the customer service field, competency means not only the knowledge to perform assigned tasks, but also the ability to build lasting relationships with customers.

- *Communication Skills:* In the last chapter we explored communication in detail. The ability to communicate effectively is important everywhere in life, and particularly in teaming—whether engaging individuals internal or external to the team.

- *Clear and Evaluating Goals:* Team success depends not only on collective motivation and competency, but equally on clear direction. What specifically are the team goals and how does it go about achieving them? Team goals must be clear—they must be understood and committed to by each team member. These goals must also be evaluative in nature—containing tangible, quantitative measures of success or failure. A clear and evaluating goal for a customer service team might be to increase overall customer satisfaction levels from 85 to 90 percent during the coming year.

- *Living Team Norms:* Norms are the acceptable standards of behavior within a group that are adopted—formally or informally—and shared by the group's members. When team members do not follow these norms, their overall performance levels are compromised. (We will expand on this topic as we explore how teams develop.)

Teams are not effective because they get lucky. Occasionally, a team may secure a "star" player who temporarily assists the team in "winning," though some key teaming elements are lacking. Long-term team success, however, is contingent on the presence of every key component.

TYPES OF TEAMS

As indicated above, we can be members of many groups or teams, both in our personal lives and at work. Here are the most typical work types:

- *Natural Team:* A team comprised of individuals who work together on a regular and consistent basis. This is typically a department or subfunction within a department. These teams are created to perform routine activities in support of the team or organization's mission. Customer service call centers are excellent examples of natural teams.

- *Functional Problem-Solving Team:* A team composed of members from the same group or department whose purpose is a problem or problems to be resolved within the group or department. This purpose might be, for example, enhancing document flow.

- *Cross-Functional Team:* Members come from diverse areas within and across organizations. These teams are typically created to develop new ideas and solve problems involving multiple groups or departments. Identification and installation of system software is a good example of a cross-functional team assignment. The duration of the team's existence is based upon the tasks assigned—the time needed to accomplish them could range from hours to years.

- *Virtual Teams:* Team members are often geographically dispersed. Modern technology allows membership from around the globe to participate on the same team. These teams can take any of the forms discussed. The disadvantages of virtual teams include restrictions associated with time zones, and limited social context. Creating team cohesiveness is thus more challenging.

TEAM DEVELOPMENT

Have you ever been part of a team that struggles with that key element of commitment? Sometimes you work well together, but other times, you bump heads. Understanding the stages of team development will clarify what happens as team dynamics change.

Diagram 5-1 depicts the stages of teaming. Let's briefly look at each stage:

- *Form:* When teams are initially formed, members are selected based upon the overall goals of the team and are then "enrolled"—committing to the team and its objectives. Standing teams commonly "re-form" when members leave or join the team.

- *Storm:* While brainstorming can be a valuable problem-solving exercise for a team, in this context, "storm" refers to struggles among team members. Storming typically occurs when there is a breakdown in acceptable standards of behavior among team members. This can be especially challenging when team members are attempting to satisfy someone's high need for power. This storming relates more to personality conflict than productivity issues.

- *Norm:* Effective teams develop clear, shared standards of behavior, known as guiding principles, shared values or, in their strongest form, a code of conduct. Some norms are undocumented and learned by team members through observation and experience. Others, such as a code of conduct, are well documented and detail expected behaviors and consequences of noncompliance. Team norms, once understood and "behaved" daily, allow the team to move forward with improved productivity and member satisfaction. (More to come on norms.)

- *Perform:* At this stage of team development, members are comfortable with one another, and storming behavior is less intense and frequent. Team member differences now involve productivity breakdowns and process improvement.

- *Adjourn:* This stage only relates to teams that were created to accomplish identified tasks over a specific period of time, also referred to as "ad hoc teams." For example, a task force of cross-functional individuals is given 60 days to identify, analyze and provide recommended solutions for a large drop in OCR (one-call resolution) numbers. While

Stages of Team Development

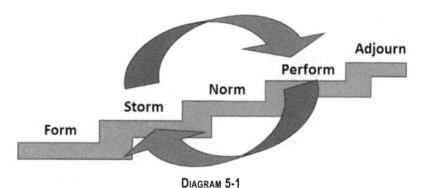

DIAGRAM 5-1

this team may experience all the normal stages of team development above, at the conclusion of their project, having satisfied their mission, they disband. It is important that the final team meeting be spent discussing their performance, covering what went well, what could have gone better and how to improve future team effectiveness.

NORMS

Let's now finish our discussion of team norms. As mentioned earlier, they can take many forms. For example, to reside on the International Space Station, an astronaut must agree to a code of conduct addressing expected standards of behavior. Norms are important because they create team cohesiveness. When team cohesiveness is high, members are attracted to one another and are motivated to stay in the group. Norms can be referred to as "team glue."

Ensure your team takes the necessary time to create its norms. A clear collective understanding of member behavioral expectations is essential to overall team success. If your team does not have norms, it is more likely a group, since it is doesn't have the bond or commitment that teams require. A lack of established norms leads to higher levels of conflict (storming) and lower productivity. Disregarding this important activity because "we all know how to behave appropriately" will result in miscommunication, friction and member dissatisfaction.

No One Washes a Rental Car

We cannot effectively create norms for a team of which we are not a member. It has to be done "by" your team, not "to" your team. The old adage "No one washes a rental car" applies well here. If you, as team members, don't "own" your norms, they will not be embraced. When you take the time to create a clear, concise, easily understood set of shared norms, the team bonds and is far more effective. Your customers will be the benefactors of that cohesion.

BEING AN EFFECTIVE TEAM MEMBER

You want all of your team members to be fully invested in the team's success—individually and collectively. As Stephen Covey said, the only person's behavior you really control is your own. Thus, while you may coach others, the key is to model successful team member behaviors:

- *Grant team members their expertise.* Each has a knowledge base that the others do not. Do not assume that you know as much as the next person about every topic.

- *Value member differences.* Every person brings something unique to the table. Harness that difference for greater productivity.

- *Focus on solving problems and not on laying blame.* This adds to bona fide learning and greater team cohesiveness.

- *Support group decisions.* While you may not agree 100 percent with a team decision, as long as you had the opportunity to share your viewpoints, align with the decision and move on.

- *Give credit to everyone on the team.* Acknowledge that each member's role is an important part of the team.

- *Be respectful of all team members.* Live your norms, plain and simple.

In summary, teams are effective when essential teaming elements are in place. Successful teams are grounded in principled leadership, and their members possess required competencies and mutual commitment through living shared norms. They communicate well inside and outside the team. Clear goals are well understood by all members and are supported within the organization.

Chapter Review Questions

1. Which of the following is not a primary reason people join teams?
   a. Security
   b. Status
   c. Sharing
   d. Self-esteem

2. From an affiliation perspective, teams can fill both social and personal needs.
   a. True
   b. False

3. A group is defined as:
   a. At least 10 individuals with a common goal
   b. Several individuals with common opinions
   c. Individuals from the same department or unit
   d. Two or more people with a common purpose

4. Which of the following best explains the difference between a team and a group?
   a. Member commitment toward one another
   b. Wearing the same uniform
   c. Working for the same organization
   d. Having a common goal

5. Which of the following are key elements of effective teaming?
   a. Principled leadership
   b. Member competency
   c. Clear and evaluating goals
   d. Clear communication
   e. All of the above

6. Team members will follow a leader who displays honesty, integrity and respect.
   a. True
   b. False

7. Ellen and Sean work in the same department. They are most likely members of which type of team?
   a. Cross-functional team
   b. Virtual team
   c. Natural team
   d. Problem-solving team

8. What is a key disadvantage to being a member of a virtual team?
   a. Difficulty with securing office space
   b. Challenges with communication technology
   c. Having limited social contact with team members
   d. Challenges in measuring performance

9. What are the stages of teaming?
   a. Storm, deform, perform, norm and adjourn
   b. Form, storm, norm, perform and adjourn
   c. Form, storm, reform, perform and adjourn
   d. Form, perform, reform, storm and adjourn

10. A team engages in storming behavior to solve problems.
    a. True
    b. False

11. Which of the following is not associated with effective team norms?
    a. Expected behaviors are documented by management outside team and given to members to follow.
    b. Higher levels of team productivity
    c. Motivated team members
    d. Increased team cohesiveness

12. Which of the following represents a way a leader can support a team?
    a. Grant members their expertise
    b. Support group decisions
    c. Give credit to the team
    d. Value member differences
    e. All of the above

13. Teams meld complementary skills and typically achieve faster results than an individual alone.
    a. True
    b. False

14. Which member "acquired need" might contribute to "storming" within the team?
    a. Achievement
    b. Power
    c. Affiliation
    d. Esteem

15. What stage of team development is associated with the saying "No one washes a rental car"?
    a. Reforming
    b. Forming
    c. Performing
    d. Norming

CHAPTER 6

Effective Coaching

Understanding Coaching

Most people have some understanding of what coaching means. Simply defined,

Coaching is teaching, training and directing.

When we think of coaching, we likely imagine supervisor-employee interchanges where the supervisor assumes the role of "coach" and the employee is the "coached." But to fully understand and benefit from coaching, we have to expand this view. You should think of a coach as anyone who teaches, trains or directs another person in any situation, *regardless of their position*. So, could an employee coach a coworker, or a subordinate coach a superior? The answer is, absolutely! How about a customer service professional coaching a customer? As you review this chapter, the answer should become clear.

When Employees Grow, So Does Your Number of Customers

The overall purpose of coaching should be to improve performance, solve problems, clarify expectations and offer assistance.

ROLES OF COACHING
In the past, the concept of coaching often had a negative connotation. It was typically reactive and related to poor employee performance, and

thus contributed to an adversarial relationship between the coach and the coached.

Fortunately, the practice has evolved in a positive direction. Today, coaching is more proactive (responsive) and tends to nurture by identifying new prospects and challenges. It leads to better, more respectful relationships and timely, needed growth for the coached.

Effective coaches play a variety of roles. Not all coaches necessarily perform all roles, and some coaches perform multiple roles in a single engagement. The diagram below identifies five common roles of effective coaching, often termed the "support and control" functions of coaching.

The Roles of Coaching

- *Evaluator:* In this role, the coach engages in appraising the performance of the coached. The process may be formal—e.g., annual performance evaluations—or informal—e.g., "momentary mentoring." For example, you notice a coworker is providing customers incorrect information for completing an online form. Therein lies an opportunity to coach the coworker by providing the correct information. It is essential this be done thoughtfully, constructively and privately, so it is received positively by the coworker. These opportunities for momentary mentoring abound.

There is an old saying, "You can expect what you inspect." If you expect your employees to excel in customer service, that expectation must be integrated into their job descriptions. A customer focus should not be assumed or believed to be common sense. Training on the skills necessary to provide that expected level of service must be followed by monitoring employee performance and providing feedback and support to further develop those skills.

- *Motivator:* When we assume the role of motivator, we attempt to emphasize or confirm a bona fide reason for doing something. Motivation techniques range widely, from rewards and recognition to punitive actions. Highly motivated employees are often eager to act. Motivation is typically accomplished through either force or influence; the former is often manipulative, while the latter is more genuine. Naturally, we respond more favorably to *being asked* than *being told* to do something. This approach creates ownership of the activity and leads to higher levels of output.

Tangible rewards can take a variety of forms and cause employees to behave as expected more quickly and thoroughly. It is important, however, that these rewards be desirable to employees.

A sales director once told me that a recent incentive program he developed had failed. The program involved a sales competition among call center employees, the grand prize being a trip for two to Maui, Hawaii. His previously top sales performer finished low in the standings. When the director explored with her how that had happened, he discovered she was afraid to fly! The reward was not an incentive to her, but she acknowledged she would have been motivated if the prize had been

87

housecleaning or childcare for a year—each the same cost as a trip to Maui.

Having realized the short-sightedness of his approach, the sales director made some simple alterations to his incentive program: He selected a small cross-section of the employees, provided them a budget and let them create two or three top sales prizes. The following year's promotion resulted in a significant sales increase. Offer employees something they find valuable and motivation will ensue.

- *Developer:* In this role, the coach works with an employee on activities that will lead to their personal development. It typically involves setting and expanding personal goals for the current year or beyond. Development begins with identifying and agreeing on one or more opportunities for the coached. The coach then monitors success, or lack thereof, with performance feedback in regular, often pre-established intervals.

In the discipline of customer service, it is important that all employees receive training on what that is and how it should play out every day. Without training, service will likely be inconsistent, leading to greater customer dissatisfaction. How many customers—actual and potential—can you afford to lose? Your role is to ensure that all service personnel are fully trained and able to live up to the standards you expect.

- *Mediator:* In Chapter 5 we discussed "storming" within work groups. Storming-type behaviors can extend beyond the group or department and may, on occasion, include the customer. These breakdowns occur when individual needs are in conflict and strong personalities are involved. In the mediator role, the coach attempts to identify the root cause of the breakdown and brings the affected parties together to seek a mutually acceptable resolution.

Storming that is not addressed will ultimately manifest as reduced customer service levels. In the long run, employees will not treat customers better than they themselves are treated. Consistently fair and positive treatment of employees translates to excellent service to your customers, resulting in heightened loyalty from both employees and customers. Everyone wins!

- *Disciplinarian:* When constructive, positive support does not work, the coach must take stronger measures to shape employee performance. In these situations, the coach identifies specific opportunities or requirements for improvement, what is expected and when, and the precise consequences of noncompliance. Since exercising this role may result in loss of pay or employment, it is appropriate specifically in the supervisor-subordinate relationship.

When a customer creates a situation that is threatening, hostile or harassing, it is the coach or manager's responsibility to immediately intervene. While "recovering" the customer may be a goal, your first obligation is to secure a safe and respectful work environment. If your efforts to resolve the issue to everyone's satisfaction are ineffective, then steps must be taken to "separate" the customer. The reality is that there are some customers your organization cannot *afford* because of disruptive behavior, and your employees deserve your full support in these cases.

QUALITIES OF SUCCESSFUL COACHES

As with any skill, the ability to coach effectively varies from person to person. Also, like many skills, it can be practiced and improved over time. Following are key attributes of individuals with strong coaching abilities:

- A strong interest in coaching, the coached and positive results
- Ability to maintain confidentiality—not share sensitive information unless there is a legitimate need to know and the coached is aware
- Excellent listening and feedback skills
- Sensitivity to others' needs and development
- Good organizational skills, as coaching is often a building-block process
- Ability to relinquish dominance and control
- Commitment to the coaching process

EMPLOYEE COACHING STEPS

The exact structure of coaching engagements varies by situation. Engagements with the most successful outcomes typically implement the following steps:

- Both parties agree that there is an opportunity for performance improvement. If there is no alignment between the coach and the coached on this basic element, coaching efforts will be futile.
- The parties discuss possible alternative solutions. It is important that both maintain an open mind.
- The parties agree on what actions will be taken, establishing expectations for both.
- A follow-up schedule is set. Regular monitoring and feedback will keep improvement efforts on course.
- The coach must recognize and acknowledge improvement. Absent such feedback, the coached is unsure if they are meeting expectations at an acceptable level for the coach.

BENEFITS OF COACHING

Employees feel valued when they are given the opportunity to develop personally and professionally. Coaching provides such a vehicle. Successful coaches enhance the self-esteem of those they coach—giving them a stronger sense of self-worth. The practice also improves communication between the coach and the coached, advancing both individual and organizational goals. When a person feels valued by the organization, they have a heightened sense of loyalty to it.

Chapter Review Questions

1. A simple definition of coaching is to teach, train and direct.
   a. True
   b. False

2. The overall purpose of coaching includes all but which of the following?
   a. Improving performance
   b. Solving problems
   c. Providing assistance
   d. Enhancing employee-coach friendship

3. Each coach must perform all roles of coaching.
   a. True
   b. False

4. In which role would a coach appraise an employee's performance?
   a. Developer
   b. Evaluator
   c. Mediator
   d. Motivator

5. Reggie is creating a sales campaign for his call center, identifying prize incentives he thinks will cause his employees to reach or exceed their campaign sales goals. What coaching role is Reggie performing?
   a. Mediator
   b. Developer
   c. Motivator
   d. Disciplinarian

6. The saying "You can expect what you inspect" refers to:
    a. Monitoring performance and providing feedback
    b. Having an employee in charge of product and service inspection
    c. Lowering performance expectations during busy work periods
    d. Implementing covert employee monitoring

7. A trip for two to Europe is always a great sales incentive.
    a. True
    b. False

8. The first step of employee development is:
    a. Establishment of a training budget
    b. Identification and agreement on opportunities for development
    c. Selection of the most skilled employees
    d. Hiring an unbiased training vendor

9. A coach may perform multiple roles in a single engagement.
    a. True
    b. False

10. Which of the following is a quality of successful coaches?
    a. A strong interest in coaching
    b. Ability to maintain confidentiality
    c. Ability to relinquish dominance and control
    d. Sensitivity to others' needs
    e. All of the above

11. Though situations may vary, it is important to follow the same coaching structure to ensure a successful outcome.
    a. True
    b. False

12. Robin met with her employee Marcus to work on some developmental opportunities she had documented for him. She told him exactly what to do and was disappointed after six weeks to find he did not complete everything he was told to do. What was likely the reason for this coaching failure?
    a. There was no agreement on the actions to be taken by Marcus.
    b. There was no apparent follow-up by Robin during the six-week period.
    c. Robin most likely did not acknowledge any improvements Marcus made.
    d. a & b
    e. a & c
    f. b & c
    g. a, b & c

13. Wes is working with one of his call center customer service representatives who has struggled to understand the company's online ordering system. Which coaching role is he employing?
    a. Motivator
    b. Mediator
    c. Developer
    d. Disciplinarian

14. Which of the following is not a benefit of coaching?
    a. Employees feeling valued
    b. Enhanced employee self-esteem
    c. Communication improving between the coach and the coached
    d. Employee turnover increasing

15. It is possible to coach customers, but it must be done in a manner that builds relationships and loyalty to the organization.
    a. True
    b. False

CHAPTER 7

Managing Change

Overview

> **The only constant is change.**
>
> —HERACLITUS

Forces—both internal and external to the organization—are constantly effecting change, and successful businesses must adjust and adapt. In this chapter, we examine how individuals respond to change and how we can assist them during the process.

Let's look at a graphic representation of how we handle change.

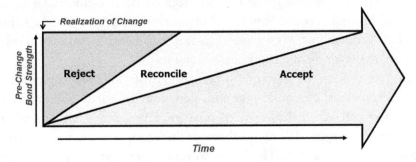

The process includes three stages:

1. *Reject:* Rebuff the change—it didn't, can't or shouldn't happen.

2. *Reconcile:* Acknowledge that the change has happened or is happening.

3. *Accept:* Integrate the change into personal behaviors.

Not everyone goes through all stages, or with the same duration, for every change. The time it takes an individual to move through the process depends upon their physical, intellectual and/or emotional *bond strength* to the *pre-change* condition. While the *realization of change* may happen for people simultaneously, *acceptance* is an individual process.

Consider the following example to better understand the change process.

Thanks to excellent growth, the Acme Supply Company requires a much larger facility for its operations. They select a site for the new building that is 15 miles from their current location. This announcement upsets Mary because she only lives one block from the current location, and now she will have to leave home earlier in the morning and bear the added cost of transportation. Steve, upon hearing the same news, is excited, because the new plant will be less than one mile from his home and will save him commute time and expense.

Both Mary and Steve experience the realization of change at the same time. Because of the perceived benefits to Steve, he may skip *rejection* entirely and move very quickly from *reconciliation* into *acceptance.* Mary may linger longer in the *rejection* stage. While she physically and intellectually recognizes the change will occur, because of her emotional bond to the old location, reconciliation and ultimate acceptance will take some time. This process may even include finding another job closer to home. There are many kinds of "acceptance" options.

Imagine the loss of a grandmother. While you understand physically and intellectually she is no longer with you, your closeness to her *(emotional bond)* will dictate the length of time you grieve *(reconcile)* and when you move on *(accept).* We all go through the change process at our own pace for a given situation. The key is to remember that *acceptance is an individual process.*

HOW CHANGE IS REJECTED

We reject change in a number of ways, generally categorized into three attitudes:

- *Did not happen (denial):* Denial is grounded most strongly in emotionality. Examples include loss of a loved one, a child born with a birth defect or a home destroyed by fire.

- *Cannot happen:* Here we identify reasons that change will not work. This might be believing a new process is flawed or that the organization isn't equipped to move into a new product line.

- *Should not happen:* This rationale for rejection is more personal. For example, Mary prefers the current work location, you are comfortable with the current work process or you fear you may lose power or status in a company reorganization.

MANAGING DURING REJECTION

Individuals in the rejection stage may need help moving into reconciliation. Here are some key efforts to assist them in the process:

- Provide all vested parties with clear and timely information about the change—encourage dialogue so they can ask questions and gain clarity.
- Let them know that the change will, in fact, happen.
- Clarify and manage the person's expectations—what will happen and what is expected of them.
- Provide an "incubation period" to allow for acceptance. Trying to move anyone too quickly may backfire. The key is to consider the pre-change bond strength.
- Listen and acknowledge feelings—avoid judging. Put yourself in the person's shoes by employing empathic listening.
- Accept resistance as a natural reaction to change. We do not know everything impacting a person—the reason for resistance to the change may not always be obvious.
- The bottom line is to be supportive of both the change and the person.

MANAGING DURING RECONCILIATION

Once a person has adequately moved past rejection, it is critical to support them as they reconcile the change with their day-to-day activities. Here are some important reconciliation steps:

- Conduct brainstorming, visioning and planning sessions. Help define strategies that will move the person forward.
- Encourage dialogue to reinforce expectations. This must include both the organization's and the employee's expectations.
- Set realistic goals to implement the change. Ensure the goals are meaningful, achievable and measurable. Goal accomplishment will generate additional enthusiasm for the person.
- Follow up on projects that are underway to clarify their impact on the change. This must include addressing process change, a change in reporting relationships, etc.
- Focus on priorities and provide any needed training. Ensure the person knows what must be done and give them the tools to do so.
- Assist with assimilation of change in daily work activities. This may include assistance with task scheduling, reorganizing work space and work flow.

MANAGING DURING ACCEPTANCE

Now that the individual is moving into the acceptance stage, it is important that we keep them forward-focused. The following steps are recommended:

- Set longer-term goals. Have the individual focus beyond next month into next year if possible.
- Concentrate on team bonding. Employ group dynamics to help those who are still in the reconciliation phase move into the acceptance phase. This can include teaming exercises, joint development of organizational goals, etc.
- Create or update the company/department/group mission statement—who you are and what you do. This collective activity not only creates a unified direction, but also deepens the team bond.
- Conduct a *change post-mortem* to identify how to better manage future changes. You can ask what went well, what did not go well and what we should do differently in the future. This can create personal ownership of future change activity.

REGRESSION

Ideally, when confronted with the realization of change, a person progresses to the acceptance stage. Again, some more quickly than others.

In reality, though, some individuals regress—go backwards through the change process. The individual may outwardly exhibit behaviors of moving forward, but physically, intellectually or emotionally, they have not.

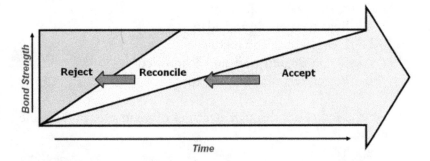

When this occurs, it is necessary to determine where in the process the individual is and to help them move forward. Leadership may not be equipped to assist everyone in every change situation. Providing professional assistance to the individual may be necessary. Some people may accept the change by leaving the job or the department. That choice can be a real win-win.

Conclusion

Change is the only constant in the universe, and it impacts everyone. Each person deals with change on their own terms. Knowing that and responding accordingly is key to assisting others move from rejection to acceptance.

Chapter Review Questions

1. We are typically only affected by external forces of change.
    a. True
    b. False

2. The three stages of change are:
    a. Reject, reconcile and adapt
    b. Deny, rebuff and reconcile
    c. Reconcile, integrate and acknowledge
    d. Reject, reconcile and accept

3. Not everyone goes through all stages of change or in the same timeframe.
    a. True
    b. False

4. The time it takes an individual to move through the change process depends upon all but which of the following types of bonds to the pre-change condition?
    a. Physical
    b. Control
    c. Intellectual
    d. Emotional

5. When rejecting change, an individual might feel which of the following?
    a. Change did not happen.
    b. Change cannot happen.
    c. Change should not happen.
    d. All of the above

6. Stephanie recently lost her grandmother, with whom she lived and who was her mother figure. Which of these pre-change bonds is most likely to slow Stephanie's progress through the change process?
   a. Emotional
   b. Intellectual
   c. Physical
   d. None of the above

7. While timing varies, everyone goes through all three stages of the change process.
   a. True
   b. False

8. Which strategies can a supervisor use to assist someone through the rejection stage of change?
   a. Remind the employee that the change will happen.
   b. Provide clear and timely information about the change.
   c. Clarify the employee's and supervisor's expectations related to the change.
   d. All of the above

9. All but which of these strategies should be used by a supervisor to assist an employee in the reconciliation stage of change?
   a. Clarify why the employee's thinking may be erroneous.
   b. Set realistic goals to implement the change.
   c. Focus on priorities and provide any needed training.
   d. Follow up on projects that are underway to clarify impact of the change.

10. Providing an "incubation period" is a good idea to allow for acceptance of change.
    a. True
    b. False

11. Which of the following is not a good managerial strategy to assist an individual during the acceptance stage of change?
    a. Set longer-term goals.
    b. Remind them the change will occur.
    c. Concentrate on team bonding.
    d. Conduct a "change post-mortem."

12. Some people go "backwards" through the change process.
    a. True
    b. False

13. Why might an individual regress during the change process?
    a. Leader is not equipped to provide the necessary change management assistance.
    b. The individual did not truly reconcile the change internally.
    c. The post-change job is not a good fit for the individual.
    d. All of the above

14. Joel now drives 30 minutes to work and was notified he would be moving to an office that is only two minutes from his house. Which of the change stages would Joel most likely not experience?
    a. Accept
    b. Reconcile
    c. Reject
    d. All of the above

15. According to Heraclitus, "The only constant is change."
    a. True
    b. False

CHAPTER 8

Critical Thinking and Problem-Solving

Overview

Critical thinkers are problem-solvers. Some people are natural-born critical thinkers. Others can be nurtured to develop these skills. The most successful people are accomplished critical thinkers, which means they have spent time practicing and enhancing that skill. Unfortunately, many of us don't give the concept of critical thinking much attention. We don't understand its characteristics, our own personal skill level or how to apply and improve it. We are, therefore, missing an opportunity to progress—personally and professionally. An accomplished critical thinker understands the organizational impact of decision-making, why it is important to use an objective process to make crucial decisions and which tools to use to analyze problems and identify criteria for decisions.

COMMON DESCRIPTIONS

Most detailed definitions of *critical thinking* resemble the following:

> **Critical thinking refers to intellectual undertakings that are clear, precise and purposeful. It is normally associated with solving complex real-world problems, generating creative solutions to a problem, drawing implications, combining and integrating information, differentiating between fact and opinion, and approximating possible outcomes.**

A more practical, reality-based definition is

The ability to combine attitudes, knowledge and skills in the perception and solution of problems.

Effective critical thinking, then, is approaching problems without bias and seeking truth (facts) without predisposition to any particular solutions. While more natural for some, critical thinking skills can be learned and used effectively by anyone. The most successful customer service professionals learn and regularly employ these skills.

CHARACTERISTICS OF CRITICAL THINKERS

The following are attributes of critical thinkers, regarding our attitudes toward situations and how we approach them. Reading this list with self-exploration in mind may help you identify opportunities to improve as a problem-solver.

- **Truth Seeking:** Inclined to seek out facts, even if they fail to support one's beliefs or self-interests
- **Open-Minded:** Interested in others' views; able to control personal bias
- **Analytical:** Apply reason and evidence; anticipate consequences of actions
- **Methodical:** Focused, organized approach to all problems
- **Self-Confident:** Trust one's own reasoning skills
- **Inquisitive:** Curious and eager to acquire knowledge
- **Recognize Limitations:** Able to reach closure in the absence of complete information
- **Cognitively Mature:** Awareness that multiple solutions can be acceptable

Most individuals possess and apply these traits in varying degrees. However, these attributes alone will not produce effective problem-solving. Also necessary are functional skills, including effective communication, interpersonal, reading and writing skills, and a solid problem-solving process. The ability to effectively problem-solve comes with time and a genuine personal commitment.

105

BARRIERS

Barriers to effective problem-solving can be organizational, such as limited resources or a climate that does not encourage or reward critical thinking. In most cases, though, the limits on effective critical thinking come from within. These barriers arise from personal attitudes and behaviors that may allow us to address symptoms, but restrain us from actually *solving* problems.

- *Mine Is Better:* Believing that one's ideas and points of view are superior to those of others, thus shutting out potentially effective solutions.

- *Limiting Options:* Choosing only one of multiple options without full analysis. This barrier results from rushing to a solution or not understanding how to address alternative solutions. As the saying goes, "If your only tool is a hammer, every solution will be a nail."

- *Pride:* Trying to protect our image when we feel we have done or said something wrong. We thus shut ourselves down to possibilities and limit our ability to learn and grow.

- *Resistance to Change:* While we understand that change is often positive, we tend to resist it—averse to escaping our comfort zone.

- *Conformity:* Rather than thinking independently, we conform to the crowd—a case of "group think." We want to avoid being viewed as different.

- *Stereotyping:* Engaging in rigid thinking about others that prevents us from considering their ideas.

- *Lack of Self-Confidence:* The strongest barrier is doubting our abilities or how others perceive them. This can cause others to delay or not engage at all.

Why people maintain these barriers to varying degrees might now be clear. Confidence will build the more one works at honing critical thinking skills. And with confidence comes the ability to break down the other barriers and better engage in effective problem-solving.

Problems

Every organization is comprised of three distinct, yet interactive, components: people, processes and things. Because businesses are dynamic, breakdowns or disconnects involving these components do occur—and more frequently than we would prefer. We call these breakdowns or disconnects "problems."

According to the textbook definition,

> **A problem is something that is occurring that should not be occurring. Something that exists because a goal, objective, desire, expectation or requirement is not being achieved.**

A simpler definition might be

> **A problem is the gap between what is currently happening and what should be happening.**

When we think of a problem in these terms, a solution can be thought of as anything that closes or bridges that gap. Our problem-solving, then, should focus on achieving the "what should be" or "desired" state. That will be the basis for the problem-solving process we provide in this chapter.

PROBLEM DISCOVERY AND APPROACH

There are several methods to determine if we have a problem. Some are spontaneous, while others are more planful.

- *Performance Metrics:* Organizations set a number of performance standards. This information is often referred to as "dashboard" data. Much like the gauges on your automobile's dashboard, performance metrics let us know how we are doing as an organization. Examples include sales, error rates or some measure of customer satisfaction.

107

When the actual condition falls below expectations, we know we have a problem.

- *Observation:* In these situations, we can physically see that something is not as it should be. This could be a backlogged assembly line, excessive employee absenteeism or a hostile customer.

- *Someone Informs Us:* When an employee, vendor or customer points out a problem, it is their understanding of the "should be" state that serves as the barometer.

- *Audit or Search:* We might engage in a review of records or conduct a brainstorming session on process improvement and discover we have a problem.

- *Intuition:* That "gut feeling" that something is not quite right, this type of problem discovery typically requires significant experience in the field.

Regardless of how we learn of a problem, the discovery is only valuable if we elect to do something about it. There are three approaches to handling problems:

- *Problem Avoider:* Despite knowing there is a problem, we continue to act as though it does not exist. We might feel it will take too much of our time, and someone else will eventually fix it. Typically, the problem grows—often exponentially—the longer it is ignored.

- *Problem Solver:* Once a problem has been discovered, it is addressed. We recognize that failure to be in the "should be" state is a costly position—one that can lead to employee or customer dissatisfaction, resulting in a diminished bottom line.

- *Problem Seeker:* The highest level of problem-solving is monitoring conditions—our "dashboard"—looking for early signs of a breakdown. Often problems can be detected and solved before they become noticeable to others. Being a consistent problem seeker should be the objective of all customer service professionals.

PRIORITIZING

Unfortunately, problems do not arise on our terms—either in frequency or complexity. Problems can be large or small; enterprise-wide or individually focused; high risk or low exposure; simple or complex; isolated or pervasive. And there always seem to be more issues than resources or time to deal with them.

To best utilize limited resources, it is important to prioritize. Prioritizing forces us to focus on the most critical tasks rather than all of the possible ones—in this case, being selective with which problems to address and which solutions to implement. As an example, we might consider the following criteria as a method to prioritize:

1. Impact on customer satisfaction
2. Cost to implement
3. Available resources
4. Regulatory compliance concerns

We prioritize or rank order by applying decision criteria. *Decision criteria* are the standards by which our options can be measured or judged. They can be either objective or subjective. For example, if we say that a computer cost us $500, that is objective—it is quantitative in nature. On the other hand, if we say the computer was expensive, that is subjective—it is qualitative in nature. Both types of criteria can be considered when engaging in problem-solving.

As an example of how criteria are established, say we want to purchase a television. We go to the electronics store and discover there are a hundred different models, sizes and shapes from which to choose. How do we pick the right television—the best solution—for us? To help us narrow down our alternatives, we might consider criteria such as:

- Screen size
- Warranty
- Cost
- Wall mount vs. stand
- Plasma vs. LCD

- Aspect ratio

It is important to recognize that quantitative criteria are easier to measure and involve less personal bias in decision-making.

Problem-Solving Process

The problem-solving process contains three steps:

1. Identify
2. Analyze
3. Solve

This may sound simplistic—and it sometimes is—but each step is important toward arriving at a true solution to our problem.

In problem-solving dynamics, there is actually a step before Step 1, addressing whether we even want to solve the problem. To clarify, let's look at an example:

You are responsible for facilities at one of your company's manufacturing plants in Kansas City. The HVAC specialist has informed you that the heating and air conditioning system is exceedingly costly to repair and must be replaced. So, our problem is a simple one—replace the heating and cooling system. But then again, maybe not.

Upon further discussion with senior management, you learn that this plant is slated to be closed in 12 months, given its obsolete technology. Is the solution, then, to fix the problem by replacing the heating and cooling system? Probably not. A more appropriate solution would be to keep the current system running as well as possible until the plant closure.

Our message here is that before engaging in the problem-solving process, we must ensure we want to commit the necessary resources.

STEP 1: DEFINE THE PROBLEM

Albert Einstein is quoted as saying, "If I had one hour to save the world, I would spend the first fifty-five minutes defining the problem and only five minutes finding the solution." Or as Charles Kettering summarized, "A problem well stated is a problem half-solved!"

If we do not take time to accurately define our problem, no amount of analysis will result in truly solving it. We may address the symptoms, but the root problem will still exist.

Writing the Problem Statement

- *What:* State the effect—*what* is wrong, not *why* it is wrong. Avoid broad categories like "morale," "productivity," "communication" and "training." Do not state the problem as a question because this implies the answer is the solution.

- *Who:* State who specifically is involved in the problem. Also state who—even if generally—is accountable for the solution.

- *When:* What is the frequency of occurrence? Is it continual or only at certain times? Consider whether the problem occurs AM or PM, daily, weekly, number of times, etc.

- *Where:* Is the problem pervasive—organization-wide—or is it limited to a department, building or locale? A key to narrowing down the problem is determining where the breakdown is taking place.

- *How:* How is the problem affecting processes or people? Use quantitative measurements such as "12%," "$5,000," "6 times," etc. Avoid loose, qualitative terms such as "poor performance," "negatively impacting," etc.

Here are some examples of both weak and stronger problem statements:

1. *Employees are taking long breaks.*
   — vs. —
   The third shift employees in the stamping department are averaging two 45-minute breaks per work shift.

111

2. *The copy machine in the Customer Service Department is broken.*

   — vs. —

   The copy machine in the Customer Service Department jams when making 2-sided copies.

3. *The monthly error rate has exceeded the allowable level because Bill is not trained to fully do his job.*

   — vs. —

   The current monthly error rate is 12% above normal error allowance.

Data Gathering

Often we have limited information when we begin the problem-solving process. At this point, we must determine what data would be useful in fully identifying our problem. Think in these terms:

- Frequencies—how often?
- Amounts—how much?
- Durations—how long?
- Percentage—compared to the total amount
- Location—where?
- Variations—from standard or norm

Note that all data may not be readily available. It may be necessary to create a report, conduct a survey, etc. in order to capture the required information. Remember, thorough, reliable data leads to successful solutions.

Process Flow Mapping

In refining your problem statement, mapping the process flow associated with the disconnect may be useful. This allows you to:

- Clearly define the boundaries of the process—where it begins and ends
- Identify the various steps in the process

- Sequence the steps in the current state

Following is a sample Process Flow Map for handling employee time sheets.

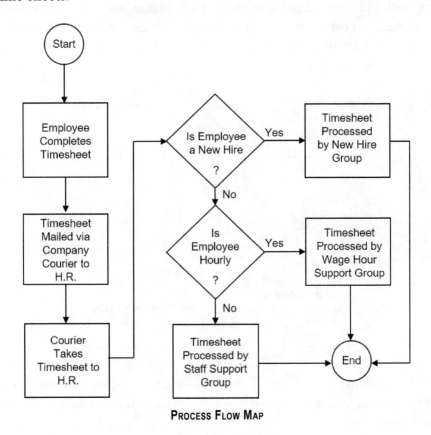

PROCESS FLOW MAP

Most problems will involve more steps, but can nonetheless be readily mapped. The Process Flow Map is an excellent visual for isolating, and thus accurately identifying, the problem.

STEP 2: PROBLEM ANALYSIS

There is a wide variety of useful techniques for the problem analysis stage. For our purposes, we will focus on several that have proven effective.

Gap Analysis

In this activity, our problem is the gap between actual and desired states. Gap analysis is a useful exercise for determining the potential cause of a problem. Through a creative brainstorming session, we can begin to determine the exact nature of the gap and its possible causes. Please use caution to not automatically conclude that "cause" ideas are correct and jump too far ahead to "solutions."

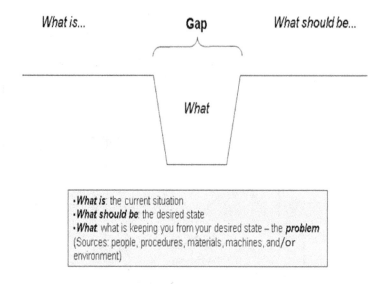

Brainstorm the reasons for the gap—what is keeping you from your desired state. These represent possible sources for a solution to your problem.

Root Cause Analysis

The key to providing effective solutions is isolating the root cause of the problem, versus the apparent or probable cause. Do this by asking yourself why the apparent problem is occurring, then why that situation is occurring, and continue until you can no longer ask why (it will become obvious when to stop). Most likely, your solution is just a "why" away.

During this process, you may discover a chained relationship (one cause produces an effect, which in turn causes another effect), so it may be necessary to reframe the problem—state it in a manner that presents the identified root cause as the problem. Please note that once a potential root cause is identified, additional data may be necessary to prove you have actually isolated the cause.

Following is an example of a Root Cause Analysis to isolate the reason customers are not providing the information necessary to process their online enrollments:

- *Problem:* Some customers do not provide us correct data.
- *Why did it happen?* The application form they submit is not completed correctly.
- *Why did that happen?* The customer said they weren't sure what to write in some of the boxes.
- *Why was that?* The customer said the instructions are not clear.
- *And why was that?* The instructions do not contain understandable explanations and examples for the customer to follow.
- *And why was that?* The instructions haven't been updated since 2008.
- *Root cause:* Form completion instructions are inadequate.

For most problems there is more than one "why." In those cases, each "why" must be explored to its own root cause. Remember, failure to identify root causes typically means we are only addressing the symptoms of the problem.

Cause & Effect (Fishbone) Diagram

Another popular method to get to the root cause is the Cause & Effect or Fishbone Diagram—aptly named for its resemblance to a fish skeleton.

Here is an example of a completed Cause & Effect (Fishbone) Diagram created to explore why nightshift error rates were higher than day shift error rates:

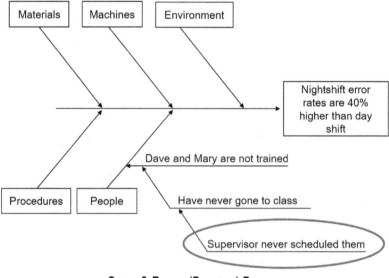

CAUSE & EFFECT (FISHBONE) DIAGRAM

As you can see, the most probable cause for the problem was circled. This is typically identified when you can no longer ask "why" in the process.

Force Field Analysis

The Force Field Analysis identifies forces that both *support* (drive) and *work against* (restrain) solving a problem. The focus is on leveraging the positive, driving factors and eliminating or minimizing the negative, restraining ones. This analysis is effective at identifying solutions in a short time. The key to this process is starting with the antithesis of your problem—your "should-be" state.

Here is an example of a complete Force Field Analysis to address a spiking employee turnover rate in a call center:

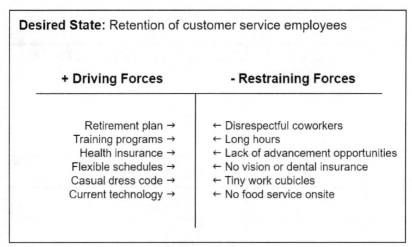

Desired State: Retention of customer service employees

+ Driving Forces   **- Restraining Forces**

Retirement plan →   ← Disrespectful coworkers
Training programs →   ← Long hours
Health insurance →   ← Lack of advancement opportunities
Flexible schedules →   ← No vision or dental insurance
Casual dress code →   ← Tiny work cubicles
Current technology →   ← No food service onsite

FORCE FIELD ANALYSIS

In this case, we have several positive, driving forces—those that contribute to the retention of customer service employees. We also have several negative, restraining forces—those that contribute to high employee turnover. The solution to our problem lies in minimizing or eliminating these restraining forces. This simple analysis does an excellent job of isolating and summarizing potential solutions.

STEP 3: SOLVE

In the final stage of problem-solving, we work to find the most plausible solutions to our problem. With a well-defined problem and isolated causes, we are now positioned to develop and implement the solution.

We may have used any or all of the above problem-analysis techniques to narrow down possible solutions.

To help us determine the ultimate solution, we can use a Solution Feasibility Matrix. This tool incorporates the solution's effectiveness rating—how much the solution will reduce the root cause—and its feasibility rating—based on the time, cost, work, acceptance, etc., needed to implement the solution.

Following is a Solution Feasibility Matrix:

Solution	Effectiveness	(X) Feasibility	= Overall	Yes or No
Ranking Scale:		1 = Very Little	2 = Somewhat	3 = Good

SOLUTION FEASIBILITY MATRIX

You enter each solution to be considered in the first column. You then assign both an effectiveness and feasibility ranking of 1–3. Next you multiply the two rankings and enter the product in the "Overall" column. Once you have completed this for each possible solution, you select your solution(s) based on the highest values. While not an absolute, this analysis does remove some of the natural human bias from the process.

Solution Selection Considerations

Following are some critical questions to ask when selecting solutions to implement:

- Do I know precisely what the problem is, what is causing it and what should be happening? (If not, more analysis is required.)
- Will this solution close the gap? (If not, then it is not a solution.)
- Are there many different solutions that may solve the problem? (If so, weigh them according to your needs.)
- Am I acting on the first solution that comes to mind? (If so, it is often

not the most appropriate one—be open to all possible solutions.)

- Have I left time to thoroughly think it through? (If not, the most appropriate alternative may not be chosen.)
- Does the solution solve the problem and reduce or eliminate the likelihood of a similar problem happening again? (If not, it may signal the need for further analysis and evaluation of alternatives.)

Conclusion

Effective critical thinking requires discipline and skills. This may be one of the more challenging dimensions of customer service. The good news is we can apply and improve our problem-solving skills by committing to the following:

- Remain open to new ideas and opposing opinions—the customer may not always be right, but they often have good ideas.
- Remain open to change.
- Accept that your ideas are not inherently better than those of another.
- Use mistakes as opportunities for learning and growth.
- Explore every option and possible solution.
- Avoid stereotypes and generalizations.
- Always look for ways to improve processes and procedures, not forgetting to abide by rules and guidelines.

Remember, the more often you use these skills, the easier the problem-solving process becomes.

Chapter Review Questions

1. Critical thinkers are problem-solvers.
    a. True
    b. False

2. Which of the following is not a characteristic of a critical thinker?
    a. Truth seeking
    b. Inquisitive
    c. Recognizes limitations
    d. Able to tune out people

3. Barriers to problem-solving include which of the following?
    a. Limiting solution options
    b. Trying to protect our image
    c. Believing your views are better than others'
    d. Resisting change
    e. All of the above

4. A problem can simply be defined as what is currently happening.
    a. True
    b. False

5. "Dashboard" data is most closely associated with:
    a. Performance metrics
    b. Observation
    c. Someone informing us
    d. Intuition

6. What are the three approaches to handling problems?
    a. Avoiding, Transferring, Seeking
    b. Avoiding, Solving, Seeking
    c. Transferring, Solving, Seeking
    d. Identifying, Solving, Seeking

7. Decision criteria allow us to prioritize our options.
    a. True
    b. False

8. Problem-solving contains the following steps:
    a. Identify, Analyze, Implement
    b. Identify, Analyze, Solve
    c. State, Solve, Implement
    d. Evaluate, Solve, Implement

9. Which of the following is a weak problem statement?
    a. The fax machine jams when sending multiple pages.
    b. The current first call resolution rate is 10% below standards.
    c. Employees are late for work.
    d. Call center employees are averaging 5 missed calls per hour.

10. If your problem area has many steps or components, it would be helpful to create a:
    a. Process Flow Map
    b. Venn Diagram
    c. Fishbone Diagram
    d. Solution Feasibility Matrix

11. In a Gap Analysis, the "gap" is also referred to as the problem.
    a. True
    b. False

12. The purpose of a Root Cause Analysis is:
    a. To identify all possible causes for the problem
    b. To identify the root cause versus the probable cause of the problem
    c. To flow the process
    d. To identify possible solutions

13. Which of the following is not a component of Force Field Analysis?
    a. Desired state
    b. Driving forces
    c. Process start
    d. Restraining forces

14. A Solution Feasibility Matrix is used to determine the ultimate solution(s).
    a. True
    b. False

15. Which of the following is not a critical question to ask when selecting solutions to implement?
    a. Do I have a general idea of what the problem is?
    b. Am I acting on the first solution that comes to mind?
    c. Will the solution close the gap?
    d. Are there many solutions that may solve the problem?

CHAPTER 9

Measuring Customer Satisfaction

Overview

As mentioned, without customers, organizations have no reason to exist. So, attracting and retaining customers must be a primary endeavor for any successful enterprise.

Besides the financial resources to thrive, customers provide organizations with valuable input. Seek and use that feedback constructively to drive business improvement and innovation and to influence your organization's strategic direction. Unfortunately, too often we maintain an "If we build it, they will come" attitude, and too often that results in failure. Recognizing what customers truly want, and more importantly, need, is the cornerstone of a successful business.

THE IMPORTANCE OF CUSTOMER SATISFACTION

What is customer satisfaction? In simple terms, it represents consumer judgment regarding the extent to which a company's products or services meet expectations. Customer satisfaction should, however, be expanded to encompass how well a company responds to consumer input. In other words, measuring customer satisfaction means measuring how well you use input to improve and expand your products and services.

Satisfied customers are important for several reasons:

- They tend to be more loyal and represent repeat business.
- They drive up your NPS (Net Promoter Score). This means that customers willingly and favorably tell others about your products or services.
- Retaining existing customers is much cheaper than acquiring new ones.

123

Research shows it costs six to seven times more to acquire a new customer than to retain a current one.

- When customers are highly satisfied, work is less stressful and you can focus on improvements and innovation versus constantly being in service recovery mode.

Learning What the Customer Thinks

There are a number of strategies to learn what our customers—both internal and external—think about our products, services or organization in general. Exploring the following popular approaches will reveal the essential requirements for securing that critical customer feedback.

- Comment cards
- Mystery or secret shoppers
- Focus groups
- Customer complaints
- Employee feedback
- Customer surveys

Note that any feedback instrument requires the willingness of those being surveyed to share their input. And beyond that, management MUST be willing to analyze, summarize and use the data in a capacity that does two things:

1. It makes appropriate improvements in processes, products or services from those opportunities identified by customers.
2. It assures the customers that they have been heard and that their inputs are being used constructively.

Let's explore each of the above approaches.

COMMENT CARDS

When using comment cards for customer feedback, it is important that the card contain only a few questions or comment areas and not require more than a minute or two for the customer to complete. A card that is too complex will result in few responses.

Additionally, businesses should consider a simple "app" version of their comment card for customers to pull up on their smartphones, complete and submit. This approach is appreciated by customers who rely on technology every day.

As just indicated, the value of receiving feedback is in analyzing and using the information to advance your business. Here is an example of what not to do with comment cards.

Recently I met with the owners of a restaurant that had only been open for two years and was losing approximately $3,000 per month. They were in a high volume area and seemed to have a large number of customers. Unfortunately, with these ongoing losses, they were on track to close the doors in the not-too-distant future.

I asked the owners if and how they acquired customer feedback on food, service and other aspects of the business. The general manager took me to a small storage room with several file cabinets. He pulled open a drawer which contained a couple of thousand diner comment cards. He then proceeded to show me several similar drawers which we estimated held 5,000–10,000 cards in total. I asked him how the information on the cards was aggregated, analyzed and summarized. He replied, "We don't have time to look at them."

So, while thousands of customers had provided feedback on various aspects of their restaurant, it was of no value to them because they didn't use it. I then shared that they probably did not need me at that time and their opportunities for improvement lay right before their eyes, in those file drawers.

MYSTERY OR SECRET SHOPPERS

Companies use mystery shopping, or secret shoppers, to measure quality of service or regulatory compliance, or to gather specific information about products and services. Many consulting firms offer mystery shopper programs. A company will contract with such a firm to provide a certain number of "shopping" experiences in a given period. The exact number will depend on the size of the company and the number of product or service offerings.

So what is a mystery shopper? It is someone who poses as an authentic customer in order to experience firsthand a service or product and then share an assessment of that experience with the company. A mystery shopper may evaluate many aspects of the experience—dependent upon the needs of the company—such as customer service, product knowledge, level of empowerment, employee training and the sales or service process. Once the shopper has completed their "shopping," they provide a detailed report of their experience to the company. The reporting format, once established, is typically compared on a month-to-month basis to identify both problem areas and what is going well.

FOCUS GROUPS

Focus groups are used to gather target audience input regarding certain services or products. Each individual in the focus group is encouraged to participate in a discussion which is pre-planned by the product or service investigator and is typically coordinated by a facilitator. Companies often use this strategy for a new product or service before deciding whether to move into the actual implementation or production phase. Because these are usually one-and-done activities, focus groups are typically not used for ongoing satisfaction measurement.

CUSTOMER COMPLAINTS

As perfect as we try to be with every customer interaction, virtually every company has some level of customer dissatisfaction, with resultant complaints. Unfortunately, unless complaints are actually received, a company may not know it has a problem. So how do we acquire this information?

While we might hope that the customer will readily and promptly share their complaints with us, this is not always the case. In fact, the unhappiest customers are far more likely to tell their colleagues, friends, family and anyone else who will listen about their experience (the story often "growing" with each telling), and never share it with the business. It is very hard if not impossible to fix something you do not realize is broken.

What is the best way to recognize if your customers have complaints? Ask them proactively! Have your salespeople and management take the time to ask customers how you are doing and what you can do to improve their overall experience.

Also, it is important to be observant. Identify if you are you receiving multiple complaints with a given product, service or perhaps an employee. These will indicate opportunities for improvement that must be addressed.

Note that customer complaints may show up in other forms of customer feedback. The key, again, is to always use the data and let the customer know you are doing so.

EMPLOYEE FEEDBACK

Employees are an excellent source of service or product feedback because they serve customers and are customers themselves. Remember, serving internal employees effectively leads to higher levels of external customer satisfaction.

Securing employee feedback can be done formally or informally. A formal process is much like a customer survey, which we will discuss next. On a more informal basis, you may gather feedback on employee satisfaction during regular staff meetings, but make sure your culture supports open dialogue. Provide a printed or online form (easily accessible and not only through management) for employee recommendations that requests the following:

- Clear definition of the problem/opportunity
- Suggested resolution
- Employee's role in the solution

This tends to create ownership in the improvement and avoids "dumping" opportunities on management alone.

For newer products or services you may want to convene an internal focus group for evaluation purposes.

CUSTOMER SURVEYS

Customer satisfaction surveys take many forms, in both content and length, and represent an excellent method for collecting feedback from audiences of all sizes. The survey instrument may be pen and paper or, more popularly, online. To ensure response rates are maximized, surveys must be easy to complete. So it is important to request feedback, as concisely as practical, on data that is most meaningful to your organization and will be most useful in improving your offerings.

There does not exist an absolute measure of service. Thus, when you hear that a company has a 98 percent customer satisfaction rating, you should ask, "Compared to what?" Survey instruments provide a baseline for ongoing service measurement. So long as the data is measuring useful information, subsequent surveys will indicate increases or decreases in customer satisfaction levels.

SERVICE METRICS

While there is not a one-size-fits-all customer satisfaction survey, certain key measurements—key performance indicators (KPIs)—are common across many industries. Be aware, some KPIs can conflict with one another. For example, you might want to have your customer requests handled on the first call and thus measure "first-call resolution." It could be counterproductive, then, to track how fast customer calls are handled by also measuring "average call time." That is not to imply it is not important to be both effective and efficient when handling customer calls. There just needs to be a focus that is well understood, communicated and monitored.

A client of ours had an objective to handle every customer call in three minutes or less. To meet this objective, they would have had to terminate calls with customers who required more than three minutes and call the customer back to continue. Obviously, this was not a well-thought-out measurement for this group, or a service standard likely appreciated by the customer. Establishing another objective of first-call resolution could raise customer frustration and ultimate dissatisfaction.

Following are popular customer service KPIs used by companies today:

- *Overall Satisfaction:* Possibly the most important metric, it indicates how customer service is rated in the aggregate. This metric should be part of every survey.

- *Satisfaction Improvement:* Similar to "overall satisfaction," but measures changes in customer satisfaction cycle-to-cycle.

- *Net Promoter Score:* Indicates how likely your customers are to recommend you to other people. The key is to get more people promoting your business than not. This is also a measure of "brand loyalty."

- *First-Call Resolution:* Measures the frequency with which a customer issue is cleared during the initial call. This is especially important as it leads to higher levels of overall customer satisfaction.

- *Customer Retention:* Indicates how many customers are coming back to do business with you again. A higher retention rate suggests a higher overall level of customer service.

- *Employee Retention or Turnover:* Remember, in the long run, employees will not treat customers—either internal or external—better than they are treated. Employees leaving the organization at an increased rate could suggest eventual downturns in customer satisfaction. Conversely, higher levels of employee retention indicate potential increases in customer satisfaction.

- *Complaint Escalation Rate:* Though employees may be well trained, there are instances when a customer service issue—initiated either by the employee or the customer—must be escalated to the next level of management. The objective would be to keep this metric rating low. Increases in escalation may indicate a need for training or increased staff empowerment.

There are many other metrics to measure customer service. Often the metrics are customized for a particular business or industry. As always, the key is that the data be meaningful and used by the organization to improve its products and services.

Conclusion

Why do we need customer feedback? Because if you don't know what your customers think about your products and services, how do you improve? "If you build it, they will come" worked in the movie *Field of Dreams,* but businesses cannot rely on dreams alone. Find out what your customers want and need (remember, differentiating between the two often takes effort), adjust accordingly and you are well on your way to becoming and remaining successful.

Chapter Review Questions

1. Customer feedback is often as important as the organization's financial resources.
   a. True
   b. False

2. Satisfied customers mean all but which of the following for an organization?
   a. They tend to be more loyal and represent repeat business.
   b. It is less stressful for the organization.
   c. They willingly and favorably tell others about the organization's products or services.
   d. Employee turnover slightly increases.

3. The only successful method to capture customer feedback is online surveys.
   a. True
   b. False

4. What is important for any customer feedback instrument?
   a. Customers must be willing to share their input.
   b. The organization must use the data to make improvements as warranted.
   c. Customers must know they have been heard and their input is being considered for appropriate use.
   d. All of the above

5. All but which of the following are acceptable customer feedback mechanisms?
    a. Comment cards
    b. Hidden cameras
    c. Focus groups
    d. Secret shoppers

6. Customer complaints should not be considered a valid measure of customer satisfaction.
    a. True
    b. False

7. Which of the following does not contribute to maximizing survey response rates?
    a. Pen-and-paper survey consisting of 50 well-articulated questions
    b. Online survey limited to a single response per individual
    c. Online survey consisting of 15 questions
    d. Online survey with an "open" period of 10 days

8. An organization that boasts a "95% Customer Satisfaction Rating" means which of the following?
    a. Not much, since there is no absolute measure of customer service levels
    b. Could be meaningful if this represents follow-up results to a prior baseline survey
    c. Most likely not compared to other similar organizations
    d. All of the above

9. Customer service surveys are a one-size-fits-all tool.
    a. True
    b. False

10. Which of the following key performance indicators most likely conflict with one another?
    a. Customer acquisition cost and first-call resolution
    b. Average call time and satisfaction improvement
    c. First-call resolution and average call time
    d. Employee turnover and first-call resolution

11. What key performance indicator would tell you if customers are likely to recommend you to other people?
    a. Complaint escalation rate
    b. Net Promoter Score
    c. Customer retention
    d. Overall satisfaction

12. A focus group would be useful to evaluate a new product or service.
    a. True
    b. False

13. The estimated cost to acquire a new customer versus retaining a current customer is:
    a. 2 times as much
    b. 20 times as much
    c. 14 times as much
    d. 6–7 times as much

14. The identity of a mystery shopper must be known to the store owner to ensure the results are representative of typical operations.
    a. True
    b. False

15. David's company is making a significant investment in time and dollars based upon feedback from a recent customer survey. Which metric would best indicate if these investments were effective?
    a. First-call resolution
    b. Net Promoter Score
    c. Satisfaction improvement
    d. Customer retention

CHAPTER 10

Sexual Harassment

Overview

Defining sexual harassment can be difficult because it is determined by the perception of the person who feels sexually harassed. What is perceived as an innocent glance by one person might be a suggestive leer to another. But the intent of the look is less relevant than its effect. If the person feels uncomfortable, they can file a claim for harassment.

What behaviors are considered *sexual harassment*? In summary, they include:

- Unwelcome sexual advances in any form
- Requests for sexual favors
- Other verbal or physical conduct of a sexual nature

LEGAL DEFINITION
The courts define sexual harassment as "Unwelcome sexual advances and requests for special favors or other verbal or physical conduct of a sexual nature."

To many people, sexual harassment means lewd comments, inappropriate physical contact or requests for sexual favors in return for job security or career advancement. But sexual harassment is often subtler.

One employee may enjoy complimenting his female coworkers' appearance when he greets them in the morning. Another might think telling dirty jokes is fun and encourages camaraderie. But such behavior can be legally defined as sexual harassment. If someone complains, your opinion about the alleged behavior is irrelevant. You may think the compliments are innocent or the jokes are harmless, but if someone else perceives them as a problem, they are a problem.

SEXUAL HARASSMENT AND FEDERAL LAW
Sexual harassment law finds its roots in Title VII of the Civil Rights Act of 1964. While this act applies nationally to companies with more than 15 employees, it is important to check your state law as it may reduce this number to as low as <u>one employee</u>.

Title VII prohibits discrimination on the basis of race, color, religion, national origin and gender. Since 1964, numerous Title VII–related cases have continued to refine the definition of acts that represent sexual harassment. The Civil Rights Act of 1991 provided for jury trials and increased damages in Title VII cases.

SIMPLE GUIDELINE
Is it or isn't it sexual harassment? Because determining if an act constitutes sexual harassment is often a struggle, consider the following guideline:

If it is unwanted and sexual in nature, it IS sexual harassment.

While the intention may be honorable, it is the perception that matters. If you are not sure, then DON'T! It is that simple. No harassment of any type IS the standard to follow.

Why People Engage in Sexually Harassing Conduct

Multiple theories exist about why people engage in sexually harassing behavior. Among the most common are:

- A strong dislike of an individual for their sexual orientation
- Predatory orientation toward others

- To gain feelings of power by threatening, bullying and sexually harassing others at work
- Ignorance of the law—not understanding what constitutes sexual harassment
- "Old habits"—not recognizing that the law and social norms have advanced

Importance of Sexual Harassment Training

No one wants to wake up in the morning and read a newspaper headline indicating they are involved in a sexual harassment claim. To reduce this likelihood, it is imperative that ALL employees be trained regarding sexual harassment and prevention principles. This is important because:

- Sexual harassment is illegal in all forms.
- There is growing sensitivity to the issue and likelihood of someone being offended.
- There are many forms of sexual harassment, and some are not obvious to employees.
- Training clarifies reporting procedures for employees should there be a sexual harassment incident.
- It contributes to a more positive, productive and respectful work environment—one that is appreciated and enjoyed by all customers.

Sexual Harassment Categories

There are two categories of sexual harassment: "quid pro quo" and "hostile environment." Let's explore each of these.

QUID PRO QUO SEXUAL HARASSMENT
The simple definition of *quid pro quo* is "one thing in return for another." Quid pro quo sexual harassment is a situation in which an employee is

confronted with sexual demands in return for something that will benefit them, such as a raise, a promotion or even keeping their job. The request may be either explicit, such as "If you spend Friday night with me, you'll get that raise," or implicit, such as "People who are cooperative get better performance reviews."

In quid pro quo sexual harassment, the harasser uses submission to or rejection of unwelcome sexual advances or conduct as the basis for employment decisions such as promotions, discharges, transfers, training, salary increases, work assignment or overtime. Note that you don't have to be the target of the abuse to be a victim of quid pro quo sexual harassment. An employee can file a harassment claim if they are passed over for a promotion given to a less qualified coworker who is having an affair with the manager.

It only takes *one incident* to get in trouble. A single sexual advance can lead to a lawsuit if it is linked to the granting or denial of employment benefits.

Quid Pro Quo Example

Here is an actual case of quid pro quo sexual harassment. A manager warned an employee that her continued employment depended on her willingness to have a sexual relationship with him. After meeting him in motels for more than a year, she suddenly ended the affair. Shortly after, her performance appraisals were lowered, and she was fired. When she sued for sexual harassment, the company argued that it knew nothing about the affair. It also pointed out that no one forced her to go to the hotel with the manager.

In a landmark U.S. Supreme Court decision, the employee's claim of sexual harassment was upheld. The Court ruled that the company should have been aware of the manager's conduct. It also dismissed the company's argument that she was a willing participant in the affair, because it was made clear that her job depended on her cooperation. According to the Court, the fact that she was fired after ending the affair proved quid pro quo sexual harassment *(Meritor Savings Bank v. Vinson)*.

HOSTILE ENVIRONMENT SEXUAL HARASSMENT

A sexually hostile environment occurs when unwelcome conduct of a sexual nature unreasonably interferes with an individual's job performance or creates a hostile, intimidating or offensive work environment.

Here are some examples of inappropriate behavior that have created hostile work environments:

- Sexual jokes or remarks
- Sexual cartoons, posters or other graphics
- Sexual innuendos or suggestive looks

A victim doesn't have to suffer a tangible economic injury to build a case for hostile work environment sexual harassment. For example, there doesn't have to be a loss of pay or promotion. Any unreasonable interference with the victim's work is sufficient injury for sexual harassment.

Again, our thoughts about whether an employee has been sexually harassed don't matter. Every complaint must be taken seriously.

Hostile Work Environment Example

Here is an example of hostile work environment sexual harassment where the victim was harassed but admittedly suffered no loss of pay or promotion.

A female employee objected to explicit photos and magazines left in plain view in the workplace. She admitted that she didn't physically suffer any sexual harassment, but she still claimed that sexual harassment had occurred. When the company took no action, she sued, claiming the pornographic material created a hostile work environment. The jury awarded her $875,000 *(Blakey v. Continental Airlines)*.

Posting explicit pornography is obviously over the line, but courts have ruled that even less explicit sexually suggestive photographs can be just as offensive and, therefore, constitute sexual harassment. Allowing employees to customize their work spaces with pictures, posters, calendars and other personal effects can help them feel at home. But problems can arise if an employee's decorations offend the sensibilities of others.

139

Hostile work environment behaviors include, but are not limited to:

- Discussing sexual activities
- Telling off-color jokes
- Unnecessary touching
- Commenting on physical attributes
- Displaying sexually suggestive pictures
- Using demeaning or inappropriate terms
- Using indecent gestures
- Using crude or offensive language
- Staring

Again, it is not the offender's intention, but the perception of the offended that matters.

Victims of Hostile Work Environment Sexual Harassment

We know that sexual, lewd or pornographic pictures, jokes or language can create a hostile environment. But the sexual comments or lewd behavior don't have to be directed at a particular employee in order to prove sexual harassment. *Anyone who is exposed* to the inappropriate behavior can claim hostile work environment sexual harassment.

Here are some examples:

- A supervisor who sexually harasses an employee may create an intimidating, hostile or offensive working environment for other employees who witness the offending behavior.

- A person who walks into a break room and hears coworkers telling sexually explicit jokes could file a complaint even though the jokes weren't directed at them.

- Flirting between a supervisor and willing employee could be perceived as offensive by another employee. This other employee could get the impression that "one has to go along to get along," or could just be uncomfortable with the situation.

Any of these situations could become the basis of a hostile work environment sexual harassment charge.

Topics and Words to Avoid

The following is a quick-reference list of behaviors to avoid, as each can be perceived as sexual harassment by the offended:

- Jokes with any sexual reference or innuendo
- Words of affection—e.g., "honey," "sweetie," "baby"
- Synonyms for man or woman—e.g., "chick," "hunk," "stud," "babe"
- References to body parts or bodily functions
- References to sexual preferences, orientation or experiences
- Compliments relative to appearance
- Crude, offensive language
- "Elevator eyes"—looking up and down a person's physique
- Others of a similar nature

    Remember, when in doubt . . . DON'T!

Third-Party Sexual Harassment

Employees who work offsite or engage with nonemployees as part of their job are guaranteed protection against sexual harassment by anyone with whom they come in contact on the job—either in person, by phone or via writing. An example is drivers who are sexually harassed by customers when making deliveries. If supervisors don't take these complaints seriously and investigate immediately, the company can be held responsible for allowing the harassment to occur.

THIRD-PARTY EXAMPLE
A female employee was assigned to work on another company's property.

She had no employment relationship with the other company and was on its premises only to perform her job. When she complained about sexual harassment, the host company insisted that she leave the premises immediately. Her employer took her off the assignment and, when no suitable alternative work could be found for her, fired her. She sued the company that dismissed her for sexual harassment and retaliation, and won her case (*Moland v. Bil-Mar Foods*).

Under the definition of third-party harassment, supervisors are responsible for preventing sexual harassment from anyone over which the company could exercise some control. That includes customers, delivery people, suppliers or independent contractors. Consider any complaints you receive about external sources as seriously as you would internal sexual harassment claims.

Remember, under third-party sexual harassment, you have to protect nonemployees on your property as well. Educating your employees is crucial to managing this balance.

Reporting Sexual Harassment

Whether directly involved or witness to sexual harassment, you have an *obligation* to take action. Silence may allow the behavior to continue. So what should you do if you are either sexually harassed or witness to sexual harassment?

- If you are comfortable doing so—let the harasser know you are offended and want the conduct to stop. This may work for a first-time occurrence if you have a reasonably positive relationship with the offender. Your goal is to STOP the behavior.

- Document the sexual harassment (when, where, who, what, time, date).

- Document your work (keep copies of performance evaluations).

- Identify witnesses or other victims (others who will testify to the facts).

- Use company channels (company policy, grievance procedures)—be aware of your company's policy on harassment—sexual and other.

- File a complaint with the U.S. Office of Equal Employment Opportunity Commission (EEOC) and/or your state's department of human rights. This must be done within 180 days of the last day of the most recent harassment event, based on your best estimate.

Under current law, the offended can charge both the *business* and the *individual* in a sexual harassment lawsuit. Typically, the business becomes the target because they are assumed to have "deeper pockets"—able to pay larger sums in a settlement. However, when the company can show it took adequate precautions to prevent sexual harassment, such as training all employees, the individual may become a greater target for the prosecutor.

Conclusion

Remember, if behavior is sexual in nature and is unwelcome, it is sexual harassment, regardless of gender or intention. It is imperative that management and supervisors work hard to ensure that their employees never engage in such behavior, and if an allegation of sexual harassment does occur, that employees understand both the legal implications and effects on morale and the business.

Bottom line: If you are unsure how the behavior might be perceived by direct or indirect parties, DON'T DO IT!

Chapter Review Questions

1. Which of the following does not constitute sexual harassment?
    a. Unwelcome sexual advances in any form
    b. Requests for sexual favors
    c. Disciplining an employee for poor performance
    d. Other verbal or physical conduct of a sexual nature

2. When evaluating whether sexual harassment has occurred, the intent of the alleged offender is a key factor.
    a. True
    b. False

3. The legal definition of sexual harassment is "Unwelcome sexual advances and requests for special favors or other verbal or physical conduct of a sexual nature."
    a. True
    b. False

4. Sexual harassment law finds its roots in which of the following?
    a. Title VII of the Civil Rights Act of 1964
    b. A company's documented policy on sexual harassment
    c. Federal case law of *Griggs v. Alabama*
    d. Occupational Safety and Health Act of 1970

5. Why do people engage in sexual harassing conduct?
    a. Strong dislike of an individual for their sexual orientation
    b. Predatory orientation toward others
    c. Ignorance of the law
    d. All of the above

6. What are the two categories of sexual harassment?
   a. Quid pro quo and situational
   b. Quid pro quo and hostile environment
   c. Retaliation and hostile environment
   d. Quo dominus and environmental force

7. A supervisor tells a subordinate that if she will spend Friday night with him, she will get a salary increase. This is an example of:
   a. Quid pro quo sexual harassment
   b. Quo dominus sexual harassment
   c. Hostile work environment sexual harassment
   d. Acceptable workplace romance

8. Once a person engages in a sexual relationship with a supervisor, they cannot later claim they were sexually harassed.
   a. True
   b. False

9. Bob tells Larry an off-color joke with vulgar language that was intended for Larry's ears only. Sara was within earshot of them, heard the entire joke and was offended. Has sexual harassment occurred?
   a. No, because the conversation was private between Bob and Larry.
   b. No, because Sara would be viewed as eavesdropping on Bob and Larry.
   c. Yes, because she was exposed to their conversation.
   d. No, because there was no intent for Sara to be a part of the conversation.

10. Steve heard Jennifer, Tim's boss, offer to give Tim a promotion if he met her at a local hotel after work. Who could file a sexual harassment complaint?
    a. Tim, because this represents quid pro quo sexual harassment.
    b. No one, because nothing has yet happened.
    c. Steve could file a hostile work environment sexual harassment claim.
    d. a & b
    e. b & c
    f. a & c

11. Staring or suggestive looks can be the basis for a sexual harassment complaint.
    a. True
    b. False

12. Third-party sexual harassment refers to:
    a. Being sexually harassed by a person who has harassed another
    b. Being sexually harassed by a nonemployee over which the company could exercise some control, such as a delivery person
    c. Being told about sexual harassment from a person who has been sexually harassed
    d. None of the above

13. Under third-party sexual harassment, it is necessary to protect customers on your property.
    a. True
    b. False

14. A complaint of sexual harassment should be filed with the U.S. Office of Equal Employment Opportunity Commission (EEOC) and/or the state's department of human rights within how many days of the last day of the most recent harassment event?
    a. 365
    b. 90
    c. 180
    d. 30

15. Which of the following is true of sexual harassment?
    a. Gender of the accused and the accuser is irrelevant.
    b. Behavior is sexual in nature and unwelcome.
    c. Complainants may file a lawsuit against both the employer and the employee allegedly involved in the sexual harassment.
    d. Due to changes in laws, periodic sexual harassment training is necessary.
    e. All of the above

CHAPTER 11

Business Ethics

Overview

Businesses with a loyal customer base are also those that behave consistently in an ethical manner. Unethical behavior can be confused with illegal behavior. The former isn't necessarily a crime, while the latter is. Let's look at two examples of business behavior:

1. Because of the busy nature of the job, Bob's Bistro actively recruits waitstaff who are under the age of 30.

2. The frontline service representative at Acme Heating and Ventilation Service often "loses" phone-in customer service requests during their busy season to meet service standards.

The first example is a clear legal violation of age discrimination in the workplace. While "Bob" may feel that younger individuals perform better in the waitstaff role, excluding anyone over the age of 30 is illegal (unless he is able to prove in court that such a hiring practice is a bona fide occupational qualification), and "Bob" may pay dearly in the courts for this behavior.

The second example represents unethical (and foolish) behavior, and though not illegal, clearly impacts customer opinion and sales revenue. "Losing" phone-in requests is tantamount to lying to your customers. Your business should always be prepared for the service requests you receive.

DEFINITION OF ETHICS
A formal definition of ethics is as follows:

> **Written and unwritten codes of principles and values that govern decisions and actions in terms of rights, obligations, benefits to society and the ongoing growth of those codes.**

A more practical definition of ethics might be:

> **Standards of behavior that tell us how human beings ought to act in the many situations in which they find themselves as friends, parents, children, citizens, businesspeople, professionals, etc.**

Thus, behavior that is illegal is prohibited by law, while unethical behavior represents activities not conforming to approved social or professional standards of behavior.

The values that typically drive ethical behavior include, but are not limited to:

- **Integrity:** Making the promises you can keep and keeping the promises you make
- **Honesty:** Being truthful—sharing facts with customers and others
- **Faithfulness:** Being consistent in your behaviors toward others and yourself
- **Compassion:** Having concern for others—acknowledging their condition
- **Respect:** Treating others in a manner that makes them feel good
- **Dignity:** Having positive esteem and bringing that out in others

> *Ethics is knowing the difference between what you have a right to do and what is right to do.*
> —POTTER STEWART

Importance of Ethics Training

Too often, while businesses train on the necessary hard skills and valuable soft skills, training on ethics is overlooked. Management may assume that ethical behavior is common sense and training is not needed.

There are several important reasons for providing employees training in ethics. It:

- Tells employees what they should do in challenging situations
- Clarifies expectations of employee behaviors
- Gives employees a reason to insist on more appropriate conduct
- Reinforces the message that the organization does not approve of unethical behavior in the workplace
- Bottom line: contributes to creating and maintaining an ethical culture

Reporting Unethical Behavior

There is little difference between observing unethical behavior in the workplace and doing nothing, and directly engaging in unethical behavior. Ignoring unethical behavior can have significant consequences on the business and its employees.

So what should you do if you observe unethical behavior?

- First and foremost, ensure you understand the correct procedures for reporting. They are often documented in the company's human resources policy manual.
- Do not report unless you are sure about the facts. Do not make unsupported accusations under any circumstances.
- Do not "grandstand" the situation—this isn't about you as the "hero."
- When reporting:
  ◊ Be impartial.
  ◊ State what happened—using factual statements only.

◊   Clarify what you consider unethical about the situation and why.

◊   Identify any possible employer liability that may exist as a result of this behavior.

◊   Maintain appropriate confidentiality.

- Finally, if you are reticent to report such behavior because you fear retaliation, you may be entitled to "whistleblower" protection. Whistleblower protection laws and regulations guarantee freedom of speech for workers and contractors in certain situations. If in doubt, check with an attorney, as regulations may vary.

Practicing Ethical Behavior

While there may not be obvious signs of encouragement to behave ethically day-to-day, you can stay on track by asking yourself some simple questions:

- Did I "live" my values today?
- Did I do good while ensuring not to do harm today?
- Did I treat everyone with dignity and respect today, even though it might have been a struggle?
- Was I fair to everyone today?
- Were my organization and I both better because I was a part of it?

Remember, customers are attracted, and remain loyal, to enterprises that consistently behave honestly and with integrity. Do what you say you will do, even when no one is watching, and your customers will reward you.

Chapter Review Questions

1. Unethical behavior is illegal behavior.
    a. True
    b. False

2. Stephen's Body Shop regularly does not return calls to customers. This behavior:
    a. Is illegal activity in the majority of states
    b. Can be cause for serious criminal charges
    c. Is not illegal
    d. Is a federal crime under the FCC because it involves telephone communication

3. Which of the following is not illegal behavior?
    a. Selecting employees based upon age
    b. Giving employment preference to a close relative
    c. Avoiding hiring any person with a concealed carry gun permit
    d. Refusing a customer service based upon unusual religious practices

4. Unethical behavior represents activities not conforming to approved social or professional standards of behavior.
    a. True
    b. False

3. Values associated with ethical behavior include all but which of the following?
    a. Situationality
    b. Honesty
    c. Respect
    d. Integrity

6. Which of the following is a reason ethics training may not be provided to employees?
   a. It is a "soft" versus "hard" skill.
   b. It is considered to be common sense.
   c. Employees already know employer expectations.
   d. All of the above

7. Which of the following is a good reason for providing employees training in ethics?
   a. Clarifies expectations for employees in challenging situations
   b. Provides employees reasons to insist on more appropriate conduct from others
   c. Reinforces that the organization does not approve of unethical behavior
   d. All of the above

8. Observing unethical behavior and not reporting it is much different than actually engaging in unethical behavior.
   a. True
   b. False

9. Which of the following should you not do if you observe unethical behavior?
   a. Ensure you know the facts.
   b. Take sides as appropriate.
   c. Maintain proper confidentiality.
   d. Clarify what you consider to be unethical and why.

10. Individuals who observe unethical behavior may be eligible for "whistleblower" protection.
    a. True
    b. False

Chapter Review Questions: Answer Grid

Chapter 1: Foundations of Customer Service

1. d
2. a
3. b
4. b
5. c
6. g
7. b
8. a
9. d
10. a
11. b
12. a
13. d
14. b
15. b

Chapter 2: Drivers of Human Behavior

1. b
2. d
3. d
4. b
5. d
6. b
7. b
8. a
9. b
10. a
11. a
12. c

13. b
14. d
15. a

Chapter 3: Planning

1. d
2. b
3. b
4. a
5. c
6. a
7. c
8. a
9. a
10. e
11. b
12. a
13. a
14. c
15. b

Chapter 4: Effective Communication Strategies

1. e
2. a
3. b
4. d
5. b
6. c
7. a
8. b
9. b
10. d

11. c
12. d
13. b
14. a
15. a

Chapter 5: Effective Teaming

1. c
2. a
3. d
4. a
5. e
6. a
7. c
8. c
9. b
10. b
11. a
12. e
13. a
14. b
15. d

Chapter 6: Effective Coaching

1. a
2. d
3. b
4. b
5. c
6. a
7. b
8. b
9. a

10. e
11. b
12. g
13. c
14. d
15. a

Chapter 7: Managing Change

1. b
2. d
3. a
4. b
5. d
6. a
7. b
8. d
9. a
10. a
11. b
12. a
13. d
14. c
15. a

Chapter 8: Critical Thinking and Problem-Solving

1. a
2. d
3. e
4. b
5. a
6. b
7. b
8. b

9. c
10. a
11. a
12. b
13. c
14. a
15. a

Chapter 9: Measuring Customer Satisfaction

1. a
2. d
3. b
4. d
5. b
6. b
7. a
8. d
9. b
10. c
11. b
12. a
13. d
14. b
15. c

Chapter 10: Sexual Harassment

1. c
2. b
3. a
4. a
5. d
6. b
7. a

8.   b
9.   c
10.   f
11.   a
12.   b
13.   a
14.   c
15.   e

Chapter 11: Business Ethics

1.   b
2.   c
3.   b
4.   a
5.   a
6.   d
7.   d
8.   b
9.   b
10.   a

Acknowledgments

First, I want to thank my partner of many years, Diane Crutcher. Her professional collaboration over the years has been instrumental in the development of our comprehensive education and training curriculum at the Center for Performance Development and the National Customer Service Association. Her personal support and encouragement for many more years has motivated me to develop this book. Without her, this publication would still be an idea and wishful thinking.

I must also recognize the thousands of participants in our training programs over the years. Their stories, ideas and positive feedback have provided us great insights into what actually works in day-to-day business operations. They ensure that our teachings are reality-based and not simply theoretical discourse.

There are others who briefly or in detail influenced my learning and teaching and thus positively impacted this book. Notable ones include:

- Henry Ford. "Yes, I think I can!"

- Professor Claude Graeff, DBA (retired). Taking his organizational behavior course during my MBA program truly piqued my interest in human dynamics.

- Denver Johnson, former head football coach at Illinois State University. He is THE role model for principled leadership when it comes to effective teaming.

- Paul R. Lister, Army major general (retired) and former president of Eureka College (Ronald Reagan's alma mater). He has been a great partner and inspiration during the many, many days we stood side-by-side teaching authentic leadership to so many.

- Gerald Olson, former chairperson of the Department of Business Administration at Illinois Wesleyan University. He was a great mentor in my early days of university professorship.

- Wes Tindal, former manager at NBCUniversal, current president of the Central Florida Chapter and chief operating officer of the National Customer Service Association. His passion for service is awe-inspiring.

- David McClelland, author of *Human Motivation* (1988). The needs continue.

- Albert Einstein. He fully understood the value of planning. "If I had one hour to save the world, I would spend the first fifty-five minutes defining the problem and only five minutes finding a solution."

- Stephen Covey. So many valuable lessons from *The 7 Habits of Highly Effective People* (1990).

- Amie and Mindie. Excellent examples of persevering in the face of adversity. If it were easy, anyone could do it.

- Nivi Nagiel. One could not ask for a more competent, professional editor and partner in this process. Your grasp of the written word is phenomenal.

- Pam Germer. She makes our words come to life through her outstanding vision and skills. I have been so fortunate to have her on our team for many years.

About the Author

C. William (Bill) Crutcher is president and CEO of the National Customer Service Association (NCSA). Crutcher began his business career after completing a tour of duty as a U.S. Army sergeant in the northern Quang Tri Province of South Vietnam. His military duties prepared him well for the physical, intellectual and emotional challenges he would face after military life.

Crutcher held numerous managerial and leadership roles in the fields of engineering, security and finance in the telephony industry for nearly 30 years. During this period, he traveled the country speaking at numerous finance conferences. He is also a Life-Certified Treasury Professional.

Crutcher obtained a Bachelor of Business Administration degree and an MBA from Illinois State University—both earned through night school while juggling full-time work and family opportunities. It was during this time that Crutcher developed his attraction to the discipline of human dynamics. This led him to become an adjunct college professor in Management and Organizational Behavior following his corporate career. He then began exploring new ways of thinking about decision-making trends and challenged himself to think differently about tried-and-true approaches. To that end, he created many proprietary managerial models and approaches focusing on a variety of topics, including:

- Employee performance
- Strategic planning
- Customer service strategies

- Change management
- Business development
- Project management

Garnering extensive knowledge through his work with organizations of all sizes—private and public—as well as his work with thousands of adult students, in both the Center for Performance Development, Inc. and the National Customer Service Association, Crutcher became equally effective in roles ranging from Executive Coach to transforming groups into highly successful teams. He has been highly active in the field of adult education since 1996. Crutcher's considerable expertise in both Organizational Planning and Human Dynamics allows him to guide businesses in achieving competitive advantage through the development of customer-centric work cultures.

Crutcher is married and has two adult daughters and two grandchildren. His younger daughter has Down syndrome, and he and his wife co-founded the Central Illinois Down Syndrome Organization (CIDSO) more than 43 years ago. This organization flourishes today and provides educational and support services to individuals touched by Down syndrome in the Central Illinois area. Crutcher continues to donate a considerable amount of his discretionary time to enhancing services for people with cognitive impairments as well as advocating for services for veterans.

CPSIA information can be obtained
at www.ICGtesting.com
Printed in the USA
LVHW050438200820
663575LV00007B/345